ROSEVILLE PO

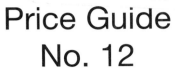

Price Guide No. 12

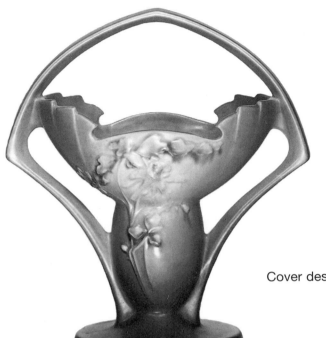

Cover design: Beth Summers

On the cover:

Foxglove, ewer, 15", #6, green with pink (shown), $850.00 – $950.00; blue, $750.00 – $850.00; pin, $700.00 – $800.00

Ixia, bowl, 6", #327, $150.00 – $175.00

Columbine, basket, 12", #368, pink, $450.00 – $500.00; blue (shown) or tan, $400.00 – $450.00

The current values in this book should be used only as a guide. They are not intended to set prices, which vary from one section of the country to another. Auction prices as well as dealer prices vary greatly and are affected by condition as well as demand. Neither the authors nor the publisher assumes responsibility for any losses that might be incurred as a result of consulting this guide.

COLLECTOR BOOKS
P.O. Box 3009
Paducah, Kentucky 42002 – 3009

www.collectorbooks.com

About This Book

This handy price guide is a companion volume to *Collector's Encyclopedia of Roseville Pottery, Volume 1 and Volume 2,* a complete listing of values for all the pieces in this two-volume set. More than 3,000 pieces are catalogued by style, color, size, and shape.

This guide reflects the most current pricing trends. Use it as a pocket guide to carry along to flea markets and antique shops.

Suggested Values

The prices in this guide represent approximate low to high evaluation. Average, if indeed an average exists, is somewhere between the two. Prices vary considerably from dealer to dealer and from one locality to another. And as always, in the end, the actual selling price is judged by the buyer himself.

There are many factors which must be considered before a reasonable appraisal can be made of any particular piece of pottery. Aside from damage incurred over the years, such as chips or cracks which obviously lessen the value of a piece considerably, certain factory defects may also detract from its value. Some of these are glazed-over chips; pieces not truly molded, leaning or otherwise slightly irregular; poorly finished mold lines; faint embossing; poor color or careless decoration. A properly repaired piece, though worth considerably less than it would be in mint condition, would no doubt attract a buyer. This is especially true with the older, rarer lines, where high prices tend to be discouraging to many collectors. Crazing is that fine network of tiny lines caused by uneven expansion or contraction between body and glaze. This is normal in moderate amounts and should not affect values unless unusually extensive.

Some shapes are more popular with collectors than others. Ewers, baskets, and covered jars bring good prices. Some collectors prefer wall pockets or hanging baskets. Generally, vases with handles have more appeal than those without. Tea sets are popular, as are tall candlesticks. Large cumbersome items which are hard to display may not sell as well as a smaller cabinet piece.

Many collectors are willing to pay more for a marked piece than for one that is unmarked yet unmistakably Roseville. This is especially true of those with the more unusual marks and is a matter of personal preference.

Examples of the fine art pottery from the early years of production are always in demand and present the greatest challenge to evaluate. Scarcity of line is a prime consideration. For instance, among the Rozane lines, an example of the Crystalis line would probably bring a higher price than one of comparable size in Egypto or Rozane Royal, due simply to its scarcity. By the same token a piece of Azurean would be more valuable than either the dark or light Rozane Royal, even though all are hand-painted underglaze art lines from the same period of production.

The quality of art work varied from one artist to another. Some pieces show fine detail and good color, and naturally this influences their value. Studies of animals and portraits bring higher prices than the floral designs in the Rozane Royal, and although any piece in Della Robbia is quite expensive, the gladiators and animals are at the top of the line. Artist signatures increase the value of any item, particularly if the artist is one who is well recognized.

These suggested values are for mint condition items. By "mint" we mean first quality ware with a normal amount of crazing and no serious defects. This definition may not satisfy each and every collector or dealer, but for the sake of establishing a basis from which one may begin an appraisal, this will be our standard.

Sizes have been rounded off to the nearest ½ inch. Shape numbers are included whenever possible; they may be helpful in ordering by mail. Many pieces shown in the catalog reprint sections of the books are also designated by numbers which can be used as reference.

PRICE GUIDE — VOLUME I, REVISED EDITION

Page 2

Roseville display sign, 5" x 8" ....$3,000.00 – 3,500.00

Page 3

Pine Cone jardiniere and pedestal,
33½",blue ....$7,000.00 – 8,000.00
brown ....$4,500.00 – 5,000.00
green ....$3,000.00 – 3,500.00

Page 4

Pine Cone floor vase, 15", blue ....$4,000.00 – 4,500.00
brown ....$3,000.00 – 3,500.00
green ....$2,000.00 – 2,500.00

Page 23

Pine Cone floor vase, 18¼", blue .....$4,000.00 – 4,500.00
brown ....$2,500.00 – 3,000.00
green ....$2,000.00 – 2,500.00

Page 25

Dahlrose jardiniere and pedestal,
30½" ....$1,800.00 – 2,250.00

Page 27

Della Robbia teapot, 6½" ....$2,500.00 – 3,500.00

Page 28

Jonquil jardiniere and pedestal, 29" .$2,500.00 – 3,000.00

Page 31, Rozane
Row 1:
1. Bowl, 2½", #927 ....$100.00 – 125.00
2. Bud vase, 4", #862 ....$135.00 – 165.00
3. Vase, 4" ....$135.00 – 165.00
4. Bowl, 2½", #927 ....$100.00 – 125.00

Row 2:
1. Ewer, 11", #870 – 4 ....$400.00 – 500.00
2. Commemorative vase, 5", # 923 ....$200.00 – 250.00
3. Ewer, 7", #828 ....$300.00 – 350.00
4. Ewer, same as #3

Row 3:
1. Jug, 4½", #888 ....$200.00 – 225.00
2. Pillow vase, 9", #882 ....$4,000.00 – 5,000.00
3. Vase, 4", #844 ....$125.00 – 150.00

Row 4:
1. Vase, 9½", #821 ....$350.00 – 400.00
2. Vase, 14" ....$450.00 – 500.00
3. Vase, 9½", #821 ....$350.00 – 400.00

Page 33, Rozane, Rozane Light
Row 1:
1. Vase, 4" ....$175.00 – 200.00
2. Jug, 7" ....$250.00 – 300.00
3. Pitcher, 5" ....$350.00 – 400.00
4. Paperweight ....$300.00 – 350.00
5. Ewer, 8" ....$175.00 – 200.00
6. Tobacco jar, 6" ....$500.00 – 600.00
7. Pitcher, 4" ....$150.00 – 200.00

Row 2:
1. Vase, 6½" ....$400.00 – 450.00
2. Vase, 6" ....$450.00 – 500.00
3. Vase, 10" ....$650.00 – 750.00
4. Pitcher, 7" ....$2,500.00 – 3,000.00
5. Vase, 9" ....$500.00 – 550.00
6. Vase, 8" ....$500.00 – 550.00

Row 3:
1. Tankard, 11½" ....$700.00 – 800.00
2. Vase, 14" ....$3,000.00 – 3,500.00
3. Vase, 5" ....$150.00 – 175.00
4. Vase, 16" ....$3,000.00 – 3,500.00
5. Pillow vase, 10" x 10" ....$1,200.00 – 1,500.00

Page 34, Azurean
Vase, 4½" ....$450.00 – 550.00
Cornelian
Cracker jar and lid....................$250.00 – 350.00

Page 35, Rozane, Rozane Light
Row 1:
1. Bud vase, 8", #842 ....$150.00 – 175.00
2. Vase, 6", #883 ....$200.00 – 250.00
3. Vase, 9" ....$1,200.00 – 1,500.00
4. Bud vase, 6", #831 ....$125.00 – 150.00
5. Vase, 7½", #901 ....$550.00 – 650.00

Row 2:
1. Mug, 4½", #886 ....$175.00 – 200.00
2. Vase, 7" ....$150.00 – 175.00
3. Bowl ....$200.00 – 250.00
4. Vase, 5½", #853 ....$175.00 – 200.00

Page 36, Rozane
Jardiniere and pedestal, 31", #524...$2,500.00 – 3,000.00

Page 37, Egypto
1. Oil lamp, 5" ....$1,500.00 – 2,000.00
2. Vase, 11" ....$1,750.00 – 2,250.00
3. Compote, 9"........................$1,500.00 – 1,750.00
4. Pitcher, 5"........................$750.00 – 1,000.00

Page 38, Mongol
1. Vase, 3"...$400.00 – 500.00
2. Vase, 10"...$3,000.00 – 3,500.00
3. Pitcher, 6½"......................................$700.00 – 800.00

Page 39, Mongol
    Vase, 15"...$1,500.00 – 2,000.00

Mara
    Vase, 13½"...$6,000.00 – 7,500.00

Crystalis
    Ewer, 7½"...$1,750.00 – 2,000.00

Page 40, Woodland
1. Vase, 8"..$1,250.00 – 1,500.00
2. Vase, 10"......................................$1,500.00 – 1,750.00
3. Vase, 9".......................................$1,500.00 – 1,750.00

Page 41, Fudji
1. Vase, 9½".....................................$2,500.00 – 3,000.00
2. Vase, 10"......................................$3,000.00 – 3,500.00

Page 42, Decorated Pauleo
    Vase, 20"...$2,500.00 – 3,000.00

Page 43, Della Robbia
    Vase, 13"...$5,000.00 – 6,000.00

Olympic
1. Vase, 13"......................................$4,000.00 – 5,000.00
2. Tankard, 11"..................................$2,500.00 – 3,000.00

Page 44, Aztec
Row 1:
1. Pitcher, 5"......................................$350.00 – 400.00
2. Pitcher, 5½"...................................$350.00 – 400.00

Row 2:
1. Vase, 10".......................................$700.00 – 800.00
2. Lamp base, 11"..............................$700.00 – 800.00
3. Vase, 9½".......................................$600.00 – 700.00
4. Vase, 8"...$500.00 – 600.00

Page 45, Tourist
    Vase, 12"...$2,000.00 – 2,500.00

Matt Color
1. Bowl, 4"...$50.00 – 75.00
2. Hanging basket, 4½".......................$75.00 – 95.00
3. Bowl, 3"...$40.00 – 60.00

Matt Green
    The Gate ....$75.00 – 95.00

Page 46, Dutch Creamware
1. Pitcher, 9½"....................................$250.00 – 300.00
2. Mug, 5" ....$200.00 – 250.00

Page 47, Dutch Creamware
Row 1:
1. Mug, 5"..$150.00 – 200.00
2. Soap dish, 3"..................................$250.00 – 300.00
3. Tobacco jar, 5", without lid ....$150.00 – 200.00
    with lid..$350.00 – 400.00
4. Mug, 5"..$75.00 – 95.00
5. Mug, 5"..$75.00 – 95.00

Row 2:
1. Pitcher, 9".......................................$400.00 – 450.00
    Bowl, 12".....................................$300.00 – 350.00
2. Pitcher, 11".....................................$450.00 – 500.00
3. Tankard, 11½"................................$200.00 – 250.00

Page 48, Forget-Me-Not
    Dresser set.......................................$300.00 – 350.00

Decorated and Gold Traced
    Candlestick, 9"..................................$200.00 – 250.00
Gold Traced, before 1916
    Candlestick, 9"..................................$150.00 – 200.00

Page 49, Creamware
1. Ashtray ....$75.00 – 95.00
2. Quaker mug ....$200.00 – 250.00
3. Ashtray ....$75.00 – 95.00
4. Mug, 5" ....$135.00 – 150.00
5. Tankard, 11½"...............................$200.00 – 250.00
6. Mug, 6½"..$400.00 – 500.00
7. Tankard, 11½"...............................$175.00 – 200.00
8. Mug, 5" ....$100.00 – 125.00

Page 50, Carnelian I
Row 1:
1. Candle holder, 3", pr........................$50.00 – 75.00
2. Candle holder, 3", pr........................$50.00 – 75.00
3. Vase, 6"...$75.00 – 85.00
4. Loving cup, 5"...............................$100.00 – 125.00
5. Flower holder, 6½"" ....$75.00 – 85.00
6. Candle holder, 2½" ....$30.00 – 40.00

Row 2:
1. Vase, 8"..$150.00 – 200.00
2. Ewer, 15"...$400.00 – 500.00
3. Console bowl, 14"...........................$150.00 – 200.00

Page 51, Carnelian II
    Vase 6½"..$400.00 – 450.00

1. Vase, 5"..$150.00 – 200.00
2. Vase, 7"...$250.00 – 300.00
3. Vase, 10".......................................$375.00 – 450.00
4. Vase, 9"...$375.00 – 450.00
5. Fan vase, 8"...................................$350.00 – 400.00

Page 52, Mostique
1. Vase, 6"..$100.00 – 125.00
2. Vase, 10"..$175.00 – 200.00
3. Jardiniere, 10"...$300.00 – 400.00
4. Bowl, 2½"..$125.00 – 150.00
5. Vase, 6"..$175.00 – 225.00

Page 53, Imperial 1
Row 1:
1. Basket, 6"..$150.00 – 175.00
2. Basket, 6"..$150.00 – 175.00
3. Vase, 8"..$150.00 – 175.00
4. Triple bud vase, 8"....................................$150.00 – 175.00
5. Basket, 8"..$200.00 – 250.00
6. Basket, 6"..$175.00 – 225.00

Row 2:
1. Basket, 11"..$300.00 – 350.00
2. Vase, 10"..$250.00 – 300.00
3. Lamp base, 12"..$200.00 – 250.00
4. Basket, 13"..$350.00 – 400.00

Page 54, Ceramic Design
1. Jardiniere, 4", without liner ....$75.00 – 95.00
   with liner...$175.00 – 200.00
2. Wall pocket, Persian type ....$500.00 – 600.00
3. Wall pocket, Ceramic type.......................$400.00 – 450.00

Dealer Signs
1. Sign, 4½" x 10" ....$2,500.00 – 3,000.00
2. Sign, 5" x 8" ....$3,000.00 – 3,500.00
3. Sign, 2" x 6" ....$4,000.00 – 4,500.00

Page 55, Medallion
Dresser set...$400.00 – 500.00

Early Pitchers
   Landscape, 7½" ....$175.00 – 250.00
   Tulips, 7½" ....$175.00 – 250.00

Page 56, Landscape
1. Covered sugar, 3½" ....$125.00 – 150.00
2. Planter, 4½"..$125.00 – 150.00
3. Creamer, 3" ....$100.00 – 125.00

Decorated Utility Ware
1. Pitcher, 7"..$150.00 – 200.00
2. Pitcher, 6"..$150.00 – 200.00
3. Pitcher, 7"..$200.00 – 250.00
4. Pitcher, 4"..$150.00 – 175.00

Page 57, Rozane (1917)
Row 1:
   Basket, 6"...$175.00 – 225.00
   Candlestick, 6"..$100.00 – 125.00
   Spittoon, 5"...$250.00 – 300.00
   Compote, 5"..$125.00 – 150.00

Row 2:
   Basket, 8"...$250.00 – 300.00
   Basket, 11"...$300.00 – 350.00
   Champagne bucket....................................$300.00 – 350.00
   Vase, 7"..$125.00 – 150.00

Page 59, Donatello
Row 1:
1. Flowerpot and saucer, 5" ....$225.00 – 250.00
2. Compote, 4"..$125.00 – 150.00
3. Bowl, 3½"...$125.00 – 150.00
4. Bowl, 3"..$75.00 – 95.00

Row 2:
1. Double bud vase, 5" ....$125.00 – 150.00
2. Compote, 5"..$125.00 – 150.00
3. Vase, 6"..$75.00 – 95.00
4. Candlestick, 8", pr...................................$200.00 – 225.00
5. Vase, 8"..$150.00 – 175.00

Row 3:
1. Pitcher, 6½"..$375.00 – 425.00
2. Vase, 10"..$450.00 – 500.00
3. Wall pocket, 10".......................................$175.00 – 225.00
4. Jardiniere, 6"..$100.00 – 150.00

Row 4:
1. Basket,15"..$500.00 – 600.00
2. Jardiniere, 8½"..$200.00 – 250.00
3. Frog...$25.00 – 50.00
4. Jardiniere, 7"..$125.00 – 150.00

Page 61, Juvenile
Top:
1. Milk pitcher ....$175.00 – 200.00
2. Side-pour creamer ....$175.00 – 200.00
3. Chamber pot, with lid ....$800.00 – 900.00
   without lid...$300.00 – 350.00
4. Pitcher..$225.00 – 250.00
5. Milk pitcher ....$150.00 – 175.00

Row 1:
1. Mug, 3" ....$150.00 – 200.00
2. Bowl, 5½" (under mug) ....$175.00 – 200.00
3. Two-handled mug, 3"...............................$300.00 – 350.00
4. Baby's plate, 6½".....................................$150.00 – 175.00
5. Oatmeal bowl, 5½"...................................$200.00 – 225.00
6. Egg cup, 3"..$700.00 – 800.00
7. Mug, 3½" ....$200.00 – 250.00

Row 2:
1. Plate, 7"...$200.00 – 225.00
2. Mug, 3" ....$150.00 – 200.00
3. Plate, 8"...$225.00 – 250.00
4. Two-handled mug, 3"...............................$300.00 – 350.00
5. Rolled-edge plate, 8" ....$175.00 – 200.00

Row 3:
1. Rolled-edge plate, 8" ....$175.00 – 200.00
2. Creamer, 3½" ....$300.00 – 350.00
3. Rolled-edge plate, 8" ....$175.00 – 200.00
4. Creamer, 3½" ....$150.00 – 175.00
5. Rolled-edge plate, 8" ....$175.00 – 200.00

Page 62, Velmoss Scroll
Jardiniere and pedestal, 30" ....$2,000.00 – 2,500.00

Page 63, Velmoss Scroll
Row 1:
1. Candlestick, 8" pr.....................$175.00 – 225.00
2. Bowl, 2½" x 9".........................$125.00 – 150.00
3. Candlestick, 9", pr....................$175.00 – 225.00

Row 2:
1. Vase, 6"..................................$175.00 – 200.00
2. Compote, 9" dia, 4" high. ....$200.00 – 250.00
3. Candlestick, 9", pr ....$200.00 – 250.00

Page 64, Rosecraft Black
Vase, 10" ....$175.00 – 200.00

Rosecraft
1. Vase, 8"..................................$100.00 – 125.00
2. Vase, 6"..................................$100.00 – 125.00
3. Bowl, 2½"...............................$100.00 – 125.00
4. Frog......................................$15.00 – 25.00

Page 65, Florane
1. Bowl, 8" dia............................$75.00 – 85.00
2. Vase, 6"..................................$75.00 – 95.00
3. Bud vases, 8", each................$75.00 – 95.00
4. Bowl vase, 3½" ....$95.00 – 110.00

Persian
1. Sugar and creamer ....$200.00 – 250.00
2. Jardiniere...............................$350.00 – 400.00
3. Bowl, 3½"...............................$175.00 – 200.00

Page 66, Corinthian
Row 1:
1. Vase, 6"..................................$150.00 – 175.00
2. Compote, 10" dia, 5" high. ......$150.00 – 175.00
3. Ashtray, 2"..............................$175.00 – 200.00
4. Double bud vase, 7" ....$200.00 – 225.00

Row 2:
1. Candlestick, 8".........................$100.00 – 125.00
2. Vase, 8"..................................$175.00 – 200.00
3. Vase, 10½"..............................$250.00 – 300.00
4. Vase, 8"..................................$150.00 – 175.00
5. Candlestick, 10".......................$125.00 – 150.00

Page 67, Savona
Vase, 10"..................................$200.00 – 250.00

Normandy
Jardiniere, 7" ....$250.00 – 300.00

Victorian Art Pottery
1. Covered jar, 9, with lid"............$800.00 – 900.00
without lid...............................$500.00 – 600.00
2. Vase, 10" ....$800.00 – 900.00

Page 69, Dogwood II
Row 1:
1. Wall pocket ....$350.00 – 400.00
2. Vase, 6"..................................$175.00 – 200.00

Dogwood I
Row 1:
1. Basket, 6"................................$175.00 – 225.00
4. Bowl, 2"..................................$75.00 – 100.00

Row 2:
1. Basket, 8"................................$200.00 – 250.00
2. Boat planter, 6".......................$350.00 – 400.00
3. Double wall pocket ....$450.00 – 500.00
4. Bud vase, 8" ....$100.00 – 125.00

Row 3:
1. Vase, 8"..................................$150.00 – 175.00
2. Bud vase, 9"............................$75.00 – 100.00
3. Vase, 9"..................................$175.00 – 200.00
4. Vase, 12"................................$350.00 – 400.00
5. Jardiniere, 8"...........................$300.00 – 350.00

Page 70, Rosecraft Hexagon
1. Vase, 6", brown.......................$250.00 – 300.00
green ....$350.00 – 400.00
2. Bowl vase, 4", brown...............$325.00 – 375.00
green ....$450.00 – 500.00
3. Vase, 6", brown.......................$250.00 – 300.00
green ....$350.00 – 400.00

Page 71, Rosecraft Vintage
Row 1:
1. Vase, 5"..................................$175.00 – 200.00
2. Jardiniere, 5"...........................$175.00 – 200.00
3. Vase, 8"..................................$200.00 – 250.00
4. Candlestick, 8", pr ....$200.00 – 250.00
5. Bowl, 6" dia.............................$75.00 – 100.00

Row 2:
1. Jardiniere, 9"...........................$400.00 – 450.00
2. Bowl, 3½" dia..........................$75.00 – 100.00
3. Vase, 10"................................$600.00 – 700.00
4. Jardiniere, 8"...........................$350.00 – 400.00

Page 72, Rosecraft Panel
Row 1:
1. Double bud vase, brown.........$150.00 – 175.00
green ....$200.00 – 250.00
2. Fan vase, 6", brown................$500.00 – 600.00
green ....$600.00 – 700.00
3. Fan vase, 8", brown................$700.00 – 800.00
green ....$800.00 – 900.00
4. Candle holder, 2", pr, brown. ..$60.00 – 75.00
green ....$75.00 – 100.00
5. Pillow vase, 6", brown ....$175.00 – 200.00
green ....$250.00 – 300.00

Row 2:
1. Candlestick, 8", pr., brown ....$200.00 – 250.00

green ....$300.00 – 350.00
2. Vase, 8", brown.................................$300.00 – 350.00
    green ....$400.00 – 450.00
3. Vase, 9", brown.................................$350.00 – 400.00
    green ....$450.00 – 500.00
    brown, with lid..............................$500.00 – 550.00
    green, with lid..............................$600.00 – 650.00
4. Vase, 8", brown.................................$250.00 – 275.00
    green ....$350.00 – 400.00
5. Candlestick, 8", brown.........................$200.00 – 250.00
    green ....$300.00 – 350.00

Page 73, La Rose
Row 1:
1. Bowl, 6" dia..................................$100.00 – 125.00
2. Bowl, 9" dia..................................$125.00 – 150.00
3. Candle holders, 4", pr.......................$200.00 – 225.00

Row 2:
1. Double bud vase..............................$150.00 – 175.00
2. Vases, 10", ea. ....$250.00 – 275.00
3. Double bud vase..............................$150.00 – 175.00

Page 74, Dahlrose
Row 1:
1. Triple bud vase, 6" ....$150.00 – 175.00
2. Vase, 6" ....$300.00 – 350.00
3. Center bowl, 10" wide ....$175.00 – 200.00
4. Double bud vase..............................$150.00 – 175.00

Row 2:
1. Vase, 8" ....$300.00 – 350.00
2. Vase, 10" ....$450.00 – 500.00
3. Vase, 10" ....$350.00 – 400.00
4. Vase, 10" ....$400.00 – 450.00
5. Bud vase, 8" ....$350.00 – 400.00

Page 75, Tuscany
Row 1:
1. Candle holders, 4", pr., pink ....$125.00 – 150.00
    gray/light blue ....$100.00 – 125.00
2. Flower-arranger vase, 5", pink...............$125.00 – 150.00
    gray/light blue ....$100.00 – 125.00
3. Candle holders, 3", pr., pink ....$125.00 – 150.00
    gray/light blue ....$100.00 – 125.00

Row 2:
1. Vase, 8", pink ....$150.00 – 175.00
    gray/light blue ....$125.00 – 150.00
2. Console bowl, 11" wide, pink ....$150.00 – 175.00
    gray/light blue ....$125.00 – 150.00
3. Vase, 8", pink ....$200.00 – 225.00
    gray/light blue ....$150.00 – 175.00

Page 76, Imperial II
Wall pocket ....$700.00 – 800.00

Page 77, Florentine
1. Double bud vase, 6" ....$100.00 – 125.00

2. Basket, 8" ....$200.00 – 250.00
3. Compote, 10" dia............................$125.00 – 150.00
4. Vase, 9" ....$175.00 – 200.00
5. Lamp ....$300.00 – 350.00
6. Compote, 5" ....$100.00 – 125.00
7. Wall pocket, 7" ....$175.00 – 200.00
8. Vase, 8½" ....$125.00 – 150.00
9. Wall pocket, 9½" ....$225.00 – 250.00
10. Vase, 6½" ....$100.00 – 125.00
11. Bowl, 9" dia.. ....$75.00 – 100.00

Lustre
1. Candle holder, 8", pr. ....$50.00 – 60.00
2. Candle holder, 10", pr. ....$65.00 – 85.00
3. Vase, 10" ....$100.00 –125.00
4. Candle holder, 6", pr. ....$45.00 – 55.00

Page 78, Futura
1. Vase, 6", #428..............................$550.00 – 650.00
2. Vase, 8", #401..............................$500.00 – 600.00
3. Vase, 8", #404, blue........................$2,000.00 – 2,500.00
    green ....$1,500.00 – 2,000.00

Page 79, Futura
Row 1:
1. Bud vase, 6", #422 ....$400.00 – 450.00
2. Candle holder, #1073, 4", pr................$500.00 – 550.00
3. Planter, #191, 7" wide......................$500.00 – 600.00
4. Vase, 6", #381..............................$400.00 – 450.00

Row 2:
1. Vase, 8", #385..............................$500.00 – 600.00
2. Bud vase, 10", #390, brown ....$800.00 – 900.00
    blue ....$1,200.00 – 1,300.00
3. Vase, 10", #395.............................$1,250.00 – 1,500.00
4. Vase, 10", #408.............................$2,000.00 – 2,500.00
5. Vase, 8", #426..............................$2,000.00 – 2,500.00

Page 81, Cremona
Vase, 10" ....$350.00 – 400.00

Row 1:
1. Candle holder, 4", pr. ....$75.00 – 85.00
2. Vase, 7" ....$100.00 – 125.00

Row 2:
1. Vase, 10½" ....$250.00 – 300.00
2. Frog ....$50.00 – 75.00
3. Bowl, 9" wide...............................$125.00 – 150.00
4. Vase, 8" ....$150.00 – 175.00

Page 82, Artcraft
Jardiniere, 6" ....$450.00 – 500.00

Earlam
Vase, 7", #521 – 7............................$375.00 – 425.00

Page 83, Ixia
Row 1:
1. Basket, 10", #346 ....$300.00 – 350.00
2. Vase, 6", #853.............................$150.00 – 175.00

Row 2:
1. Rose bowl, 4", #326 ....$150.00 – 175.00
2. Bowl, 6", #327 ....$150.00 – 175.00

Page 85, Clemana
Vase, 7", #123, blue.............................$350.00 – 400.00
green...$300.00 – 350.00
tan...$250.00 – 300.00
Candle holders, #1104, 4½", pr., blue ....$325.00 – 375.00
green...$300.00 – 325.00
tan...$275.00 – 325.00

Page 85, Sunflower
Row 1:
1. Vase, 5½", #488 ....$1,100.00 – 1,300.00
2. Vase, 8", #491 ....$1,700.00 – 1,900.00
3. Vase, 7", #487 ....$1,000.00 – 1,200.00
4. Vase, 6", #485 ....$650.00 –750.00

Row 2:
1. Vase, 10", #493..............................$1,500.00 – 1,700.00
2. Jardiniere, 9", #619 ....$2,000.00 – 2,500.00
3. Vase, 8", #490...............................$1,500.00 – 1,700.00

Page 87, Thorn Apple
Row 1:
1. Cornucopia vase, 6", #127 ....$150.00 – 175.00
2. Planter, 5", #262...........................$150.00 – 175.00
3. Vase, 6", #812...............................$150.00 – 175.00

Row 2:
1. Candle holder, 2½", #1117, pr. ....$200.00 – 225.00
2. Candle holder, 5½", #1118, pr. ....$300.00 – 350.00

Row 3:
1. Vase, 4", #808...............................$150.00 – 175.00
2. Basket, 10", #342 ....$350.00 – 400.00
3. Vase, 4", #808...............................$150.00 – 175.00

Page 89, Iris
Row 1:
1. Bowl, 6", #360, blue.........................$200.00 – 250.00
   pink or tan..................................$175.00 – 225.00
2. Wall shelf, 8", #2, blue ....$500.00 – 550.00
   pink or tan..................................$450.00 – 500.00
3. Jardiniere, 5", #647, blue.................$200.00 – 250.00
   pink or tan..................................$175.00 – 225.00

Row 2:
1. Vase, 4", #914, blue.........................$125.00 – 150.00
   pink or tan..................................$100.00 – 125.00
2. Center bowl, 14", #364, blue.................$300.00 – 350.00
   pink or tan..................................$250.00 – 300.00
3. Candle holders, 4", #1135, pr., blue .....$300.00 – 350.00
   pink or tan..................................$250.00 – 300.00

Row 3:
1. Ewer, 10", #926, blue.............................$350.00 – 400.00
   pink or tan..................................$250.00 – 300.00
2. Basket, 8", #354, blue ....$400.00 – 450.00
   pink or tan..................................$350.00 – 400.00

Page 91, Poppy
Row 1:
1. Wall pocket candle holder, 9",
   #1281, pink ....$900.00 – 1,000.00
   gray or green................................$800.00 – 900.00
2. Vase, 6½", #867.............................$175.00 – 200.00
   gray or green................................$125.00 – 150.00

Row 2:
1. Ewer, 10", #876, pink ....$450.00 – 550.00
   gray or green................................$375.00 – 450.00
2. Basket, 10", #347, pink........................$450.00 – 550.00
   gray or green................................$375.00 – 450.00

Page 93, Moss
Row 1:
Candlesticks, 4½", #1107, pink & green ....$275.00 – 325.00
   orange & green..................................$275.00 – 325.00
   blue ....$200.00 – 225.00

Row 2:
1. Vase, 6", #744, pink & green ....$225.00 – 250.00
   orange & green..................................$225.00 – 250.00
   blue ....$175.00 – 200.00
2. Vase, 8", #779, pink & green ....$450.00 – 500.00
   orange & green..................................$450.00 – 500.00
   blue ....$375.00 – 425.00

Row 3:
Center bowl, 12", #294, pink & green ....$300.00 – 350.00
   orange & green..................................$300.00 – 350.00
   blue ....$225.00 – 250.00

Page 94, Ferella
1. Vase, 4", #497, red.............................$475.00 – 525.00
   tan ....$400.00 – 450.00
2. Vase, 9", #507, red...........................$1,500.00 – 1,750.00
   tan ....$800.00 – 900.00
3. Bowl, 12", #212, red ....$1,100.00 – 1,300.00
   tan ....$900.00 – 1,100.00
4. Vase, 6", #502, red ....$750.00 – 850.00
   tan ....$600.00 – 700.00
5. Vase, 9, #510, red ....$1,750.00 – 2,000.00
   tan ....$1,250.00 – 1,500.00

Page 95, Falline
1. Vase, 6", #644, blue...........................$1,300.00 – 1,500.00
   tan ....$600.00 – 700.00
2. Vase, 8", #649, blue...........................$1,500.00 – 1,750.00
   tan ....$800.00 – 900.00
3. Lamp, 6½", #650, tan $500.00
   blue ....$1,500.00 – 1,700.00
   tan ....$800.00 – 900.00
4. Vase, 6½", #645, blue.......................$1,300.00 – 1,500.00
   tan ....$700.00 – 800.00

5. Vase, 6", #643, blue ....$1,000.00 – 1,100.00
    tan ....$600.00 – 700.00

Tourmaline
    Ginger jar, 9" ....$400.00 – 450.00

Row 1:
1. Rose bowl, 5", #238 ....$75.00 – 100.00
2. Vase, 8", #613 ....$125.00 – 150.00
3. Frog ....$30.00 – 40.00

Row 2:
1. Vase, 6", #A-517 ....$75.00 – 100.00
2. Center bowl, 5" x 12½", #241 ....$175.00 – 225.00
3. Vase, 6", #679 ....$75.00 – 100.00

Page 97, Montacello
Row 1:
1. Vase, 4", #555, blue ....$375.00 – 425.00
    tan ....$350.00 – 375.00
2. Basket, 6½", #333, blue ....$1,200.00 – 1,400.00
    tan ....$900.00 – 1,000.00
3. Vase, 5", #555, blue ....$375.00 – 425.00
    tan ....$350.00 – 375.00

Row 2:
1. Vase, 6", extreme right and left,
    #560, blue ....$600.00 – 700.00
    tan ....$500.00 – 600.00
2. Vase, 7", #561, blue ....$750.00 – 850.00
    tan ....$600.00 – 700.00

Row 3:
1. Vase, extreme right and left, 7",
    #561, blue ....$750.00 – 850.00
    tan ....$600.00 – 700.00
2. Vase, 9", #564, blue......................$1,300.00 – 1,500.00
    tan ....$900.00 – 1,100.00

Page 99, Windsor
Row 1:
1. Candlesticks, 4½", #1084, pr., blue........$550.00 – 650.00
    tan ....$450.00 – 550.00
2. Vase, 5", #545, blue ....$450.00 – 550.00
    tan ....$400.00 – 450.00

Row 2:
1. Vase, 5", #545, blue ....$450.00 – 500.00
    tan ....$400.00 – 500.00
2. Center bowl, 16" wide, #224, blue ....$500.00 – 600.00
    tan ....$400.00 – 500.00
3. Frog, blue ....$50.00 – 75.00
    tan ....$50.00 – 75.00

Row 3:
1. Vase, 7", #549, blue ....$1,100.00 – 1,300.00
    tan ....$900.00 – 1,100.00
2. Vase, 9", #582, blue ....$1,500.00 – 1,750.00
    tan ....$1,000.00 – 1,250.00
3. Vase, 7", #549, blue ....$1,100.00 – 1,300.00
    tan ....$900.00 – 1,100.00

Page 101, Cosmos
Row 1:
1. Vase, 4", #944, blue ....$150.00 – 175.00
    green ....$125.00 – 150.00
    tan ....$100.00 – 125.00
2. Bowl Vase, 6", #376, blue....................$375.00 – 425.00
    green ....$325.00 – 375.00
    tan ....$250.00 – 300.00
3. Vase, 3", #649, blue ....$150.00 – 175.00
    green ....$125.00 – 150.00
    tan ....$100.00 – 125.00

Row 2:
1. Basket, 12", #358, blue ....$500.00 – 550.00
    green ....$450.00 – 500.00
    tan ....$400.00 – 450.00
2. Candle holder, 2½", #1137, pr., blue ......$275.00 – 300.00
    green ....$250.00 – 275.00
    tan ....$225.00 – 250.00
3. Ewer, 15", #957, blue......................$1,100.00 – 1,200.00
    green ....$1,000.00 – 1,100.00
    tan ....$900.00 – 1,000.00

Page 103, Jonquil
Row 1:
1. Vase, 4", #539 ....$175.00 – 225.00
2. Basket, 9", #324 ....$600.00 – 700.00
3. Bud vase, 7", #102 ....$350.00 – 400.00
4. Bowl, 4", #538 ....$200.00 – 250.00

Row 2:
1. Vase, 8", #527 ....$400.00 – 450.00
2. Basket, 10", #328 ....$800.00 – 900.00
3. Jardiniere, 6", #621 ....$300.00 – 350.00

Page 105, Blackberry
Row 1:
1. Vase, 5", #569 ....$500.00 – 600.00
2. Vase, 4", #567 ....$450.00 – 500.00
3. Vase, 6", #572 ....$650.00 – 700.00
4. Wall pocket, #1267 ....$2,000.00 – 2,500.00
5. Bowl, 6" wide, #226 ....$450.00 – 500.00

Row 2:
1. Vase, 6", #574 ....$700.00 – 800.00
2. Jardiniere, 6", #623 ....$550.00 – 650.00
3. Vase, 6", #573 ....$650.00 – 700.00
4. Vase, 5", #570 ....$500.00 – 600.00

Row 3:
1. Candle holders, 4½", pr., #1086 ....$700.00 – 800.00
2. Center bowl, 13" wide, #228 ....$700.00 – 800.00
3. Vase, 4", #568 ....$500.00 – 550.00

Row 4:
1. Vase, 8", #576 ....$850.00 – 950.00
2. Vase, 10", #577 ....$1,500.00 – 1,750.00
3. Vase, 12½", #578 ....$2,000.00 – 2,500.00
4. Vase, 8", #575 ....$750.00 – 850.00

Page 107, Cherry Blossom
Row 1:
1. Candle holders, 4", pr., #1090, brown....$500.00 – 550.00
   pink & blue ....$750.00 – 850.00
2. Bowl vase, 6", #621, brown.....................$450.00 – 500.00
   pink & blue ....$650.00 – 750.00
3. Jardiniere, 5", #627, brown......................$325.00 – 375.00
   pink & blue ....$475.00 – 525.00

Row 2:
1. Vase, 5", #619, brown..............................$350.00 – 400.00
   pink & blue ....$550.00 – 600.00
2. Vase, 7½", #620, brown...........................$375.00 – 425.00
   pink & blue ....$550.00 – 600.00
3. Vase, 10", #626, brown............................$650.00 – 750.00
   pink & blue ....$1,100.00 – 1,200.00
4. Vase, 7", #622, brown..............................$450.00 – 500.00
   pink & blue ....$650.00 – 750.00

Row 3:
1. Vase, 5", #619, brown..............................$350.00 – 400.00
   pink & blue ....$550.00 – 600.00
2. Vase, 7", #623, brown..............................$500.00 – 550.00
   pink & blue ....$750.00 – 850.00
3. Vase, 8", #624, brown..............................$550.00 – 600.00
   pink & blue ....$900.00 – 1,000.00
4. Vase, 7", #622, brown..............................$500.00 – 550.00
   pink & blue ....$750.00 – 850.00
5. Vase, 4", #617, brown..............................$325.00 – 375.00
   pink & blue ....$500.00 – 550.00

Row 4:
1. Factory lamp base, brown ....$1,250.00 – 1,500.00
   pink & blue ....$2,000.00 – 2,500.00
2. Jardiniere, 10", #627, brown............$1,250.00 – 1,500.00
   pink & blue ....$2,000.00 – 2,500.00
3. Vase, 8", #625, brown..........................$650.00 – 750.00
   pink & blue ....$1,100.00 – 1,200.00

Page 108, Baneda
Row 1:
1. Vase, 5½", #601, pink ....$450.00 – 500.00
   green ....$600.00 – 650.00
2. Candle holder, 4½", #1088, pr., pink ......$650.00 – 750.00
   green ....$850.00 – 950.00
3. Center bowl, 13" across, #237, pink ......$750.00 – 900.00
   green ....$900.00 – 1,100.00
4. Vase, 6", #588, pink ....$500.00 – 550.00
   green ....$600.00 – 650.00

Row 2:
1. Vase, 8", #593, pink ....$700.00 – 800.00
   green ....$900.00 – 1,000.00
2. Jardiniere, 9½", #626, pink ....$1,800.00 – 2,000.00
   green ....$2,500.00 – 2,750.00
3. Vase, 8", #593, pink ....$700.00 – 800.00
   green ....$900.00 – 1,000.00

Page 109, Wisteria
Row 1:
1. Center bowl, 12", #423, tan....................$500.00 – 550.00

blue ....$850.00 – 950.00
2. Vase, 7", #634, tan..................................$550.00 – 600.00
   blue ....$850.00 – 950.00
3. Vase, 6", #631, tan..................................$400.00 – 450.00
   blue ....$600.00 – 650.00
4. Bowl, 4", #242, tan..................................$350.00 – 400.00
   blue ....$500.00 – 550.00

Row 2:
1. Vase, 8", #633, tan..................................$650.00 – 700.00
   blue ....$900.00 – 1,000.00
2. Vase, 9", #681, tan..............................$900.00 – 1,000.00
   blue ....$1,500.00 – 1,750.00
3. Vase, 10", #639, tan...........................$900.00 – 1,000.00
   blue ....$1,500.00 – 1,750.00
4. Vase, 6", #637, tan..................................$800.00 – 900.00
   blue ....$1,400.00 – 1,600.00

Page 110, Laurel
Row 1:
1. Bowl, 7" wide, #251, gold.......................$250.00 – 275.00
   russet ....$275.00 – 300.00
   green ....$300.00 – 325.00
2. Vase, 7", #670, gold................................$325.00 – 350.00
   russet ....$350.00 – 375.00
   green ....$400.00 – 450.00
3. Vase, 6½", #669, gold.............................$300.00 – 325.00
   russet ....$325.00 – 350.00
   green ....$375.00 – 425.00
4. Vase, 6", #667, gold................................$275.00 – 300.00
   russet ....$300.00 – 325.00
   green ....$350.00 – 375.00

Row 2:
1. Vase, 8", #671, gold................................$350.00 – 375.00
   russet ....$400.00 – 450.00
   green ....$450.00 – 500.00
2. Vase, 9", #675, gold................................$550.00 – 600.00
   russet ....$600.00 – 700.00
   green ....$700.00 – 800.00
3. Vase, 8½", #672, gold.............................$500.00 – 550.00
   russet ....$550.00 – 650.00
   green ....$650.00 – 750.00
4. Vase, 6", #668, gold................................$250.00 – 275.00
   russet ....$275.00 – 300.00
   green ....$300.00 – 325.00

Page 111, Luffa
1. Jardiniere, 4", #631 ....$400.00 – 450.00
2. Vase, 7", #685..$550.00 – 650.00
3. Vase, 12", #691 ....$1,000.00 – 1,200.00
4. Vase, 7", #685..$550.00 – 650.00
5. Vase, 6", #684..$450.00 – 550.00

Page 112, Primrose
1. Vase, 8", #767, blue or pink....................$350.00 – 400.00
   tan ....$275.00 – 325.00
2. Bowl, 4", #284, blue or pink ....$250.00 – 275.00
   tan ....$200.00 – 225.00
3. Vase, 8", #765, blue or pink....................$325.00 – 375.00
   tan ....$250.00 – 275.00

Page 113, Topeo
	Vase, 9½", #662, blue	$450.00 – 500.00
	red	$275.00 – 325.00
1.	Vase, 7", #658, blue	$400.00 – 450.00
	red	$225.00 – 275.00
2.	Vase, 9", #661, blue	$600.00 – 700.00
	red	$400.00 – 500.00

Row 1:
| | Bowl, 2½", blue | $225.00 – 250.00 |
| | red | $150.00 – 175.00 |

Row 2:
1.	Vase, 6", #245, blue	$450.00 – 550.00
	red	$300.00 – 325.00
2.	Vase, 6½", #656, blue	$400.00 – 450.00
	red	$175.00 – 200.00

Page 115, Pine Cone
Row 1:
1.	Triple candle holders, 5½", #1106, green	$500.00 – 600.00
	brown	$700.00 – 800.00
	blue	$900.00 – 1,000.00
2.	Bowl, 3", #632, green	$125.00 – 150.00
	brown	$150.00 – 175.00
	blue	$175.00 – 225.00
3.	Basket/planter, 3½", #468, green	$350.00 – 400.00
	brown	$475.00 – 525.00
	blue	$675.00 – 750.00
4.	Planter, 6", #456, green	$200.00 – 250.00
	brown	$250.00 – 300.00
	blue	$300.00 – 350.00
5.	Basket, 6", #408, green	$350.00 – 400.00
	brown	$450.00 – 500.00
	blue	$650.00 – 750.00

Row 2:
1.	Fan vase, 6", #472, green	$350.00 – 400.00
	brown	$450.00 – 500.00
	blue	$650.00 – 750.00
2.	Center bowl, 15" wide, #323, green	$350.00 – 400.00
	brown	$450.00 – 500.00
	blue	$650.00 – 750.00
3.	Cornucopia, 8", #128, green	$200.00 – 250.00
	brown	$250.00 – 300.00
	blue	$400.00 – 450.00

Row 3:
1.	Ice-lip pitcher, 8", #1321, green	$375.00 – 450.00
	brown	$550.00 – 600.00
	blue	$900.00 – 1,000.00
2.	Cornucopia, 6", #126, green	$175.00 – 225.00
	brown	$225.00 – 275.00
	blue	$350.00 – 400.00
3.	Basket, 10", #410, green	$425.00 – 475.00
	brown	$500.00 – 550.00
	blue	$950.00 – 1,100.00
4.	Pitcher, 9", #425, green	$550.00 – 650.00
	brown	$750.00 – 850.00
	blue	$1,000.00 – 1,250.00

Row 4:
1.	Vase, 10", #709, green	$375.00 – 425.00
	brown	$450.00 – 500.00
	blue	$800.00 – 900.00
2.	Basket, 9" x 13", #339, green	$500.00 – 600.00
	brown	$650.00 – 750.00
	blue	$1,100.00 – 1,300.00
3.	Vase, 7", #112, green	$175.00 – 200.00
	brown	$250.00 – 275.00
	blue	$400.00 – 450.00
4.	Basket 10", #338, green	$400.00 – 450.00
	brown	$500.00 – 550.00
	blue	$850.00 – 950.00

Page 116, Velmoss
1.	Vase, 7", #716, green	$200.00 – 250.00
	blue	$300.00 – 350.00
	red	$350.00 – 400.00
	tan (rare)	$400.00 – 450.00
2.	Double bud vase, 8", #116, green	$200.00 – 250.00
	blue	$300.00 – 350.00
	red	$350.00 – 400.00
	tan (rare)	$400.00 – 450.00
3.	Vase, 6", #714, green	$150.00 – 200.00
	blue	$275.00 – 325.00
	red	$325.00 – 375.00
	tan (rare)	$375.00 – 425.00

Page 117, Velmoss
1.	Double cornucopia, 8½", #117, green	$200.00 – 225.00
	blue	$375.00 – 425.00
	red	$425.00 – 475.00
	tan (rare)	$475.00 – 525.00

Russco
1.	Bud vase, 8", #695	$175.00 – 200.00
2.	Vase, 6", #259	$300.00 – 350.00
3.	Vase, 15", #703	$250.00 – 300.00
4.	Vase, 6½", #259	$125.00 – 150.00

Page 118, Orian
1.	Vase, 7", #735, tan	$200.00 – 250.00
	turquoise	$225.00 – 275.00
	yellow	$250.00 – 300.00
	red	$325.00 – 375.00
2.	Vase, 8", #736, tan	$250.00 – 300.00
	turquoise	$275.00 – 325.00
	yellow	$350.00 – 400.00
	red	$400.00 – 450.00
3.	Vase, 12", #742, tan	$400.00 – 450.00
	turquoise	$425.00 – 475.00
	yellow	$475.00 – 525.00
	red	$525.00 – 600.00
4.	Bowl vase, 6", #274, tan	$350.00 – 400.00
	turquoise	$375.00 – 425.00
	yellow	$425.00 – 475.00
	red	$475.00 – 525.00

Page 119, Teasel
Row 1
1. Vase, 5", #644, dark blue or rust ....$200.00 – 225.00
   light blue or tan ....$175.00 – 200.00
2. Vase, 6", #34, dark blue or rust ....$250.00 – 300.00
   light blue or tan ....$200.00 – 250.00
3. Vase, 6", #882, dark blue or rust ....$200.00 – 225.00
   light blue or tan ....$175.00 – 200.00
4. Bowl, 4", #342, dark blue or rust ....$200.00 – 225.00
   light blue or tan ....$175.00 – 200.00

Row 2:
1. Basket, 10", #349, dark blue or rust.......$700.00 – 750.00
   light blue or tan ....$600.00 – 650.00
2. Ewer, 18", #890, dark blue or rust ....$850.00 – 950.00
   light blue or tan ....$700.00 – 800.00
3. Basket, 10", #349, dark blue or rust.......$700.00 – 750.00
   light blue or tan ....$600.00 – 650.00

Page 120, Morning Glory
Row 1:
1. Bowl Vase, 4", #268, green.....................$450.00 – 500.00
   ivory..$350.00 – 400.00
2. Vase, 6", #269, green.............................$800.00 – 900.00
   ivory..$500.00 – 600.00
3. Vase, 7", #725, green.............................$650.00 – 750.00
   ivory..$450.00 – 500.00
4. Vase, 6", #724, green.............................$450.00 – 500.00
   ivory..$350.00 – 400.00

Row 2:
1. Vase, 8", #727, green............................$750.00 – 800.00
   ivory..$550.00 – 600.00
2. Vase, 12", #731, green.................$1,750.00 – 2,000.00
   ivory..$1,000.00 – 1,100.00
3. Vase, 10", #730, green..........................$950.00 – 1,150.00
   ivory..$650.00 – 700.00

Page 121, Moderne
1. Lamp, 9", #799 ....$400.00 – 450.00
   Vase only, 9", #799 ....$750.00 – 850.00
2. Vase, 7", #794 ....$175.00 – 200.00

Dawn
1. Vase, 6", #827, pink or yellow ....$200.00 – 250.00
   green ....$175.00 – 200.00
2. Vase, 8", #828, pink or yellow ....$300.00 – 350.00
   green ....$250.00 – 275.00
3. Vase, 6", #826, pink or yellow ....$200.00 – 250.00
   green ....$175.00 – 200.00

Page 122, Rozane Pattern
1. Bud vase, 6", #2 ....$125.00 – 150.00
2. Planter, 14" wide, #397 ....$150.00 – 175.00
3. Vase, 6", #398 ....$150.00 – 175.00

Page 123, Fuchsia
Row 1:
Ice-lip pitcher, 8", #1322, blue................$750.00 – 850.00
   green ....$550.00 – 625.00
   tan ....$475.00 – 525.00

Row 2:
1. Bowl vase, 4", #346, blue ....$200.00 – 225.00
   green ....$175.00 – 200.00
   tan ....$150.00 – 175.00
2. Jardiniere, 3", #645, blue ....$150.00 – 175.00
   green ....$125.00 – 150.00
   tan ....$100.00 – 125.00

Row 3:
1. Vase, 7", #895, blue ....$350.00 – 400.00
   green ....$300.00 – 350.00
   tan ....$250.00 – 300.00
2. Vase, 12", #903, blue ....$850.00 – 950.00
   green ....$650.00 – 750.00
   tan ....$550.00 – 650.00
3. Basket and frog, 8", #350, blue..............$700.00 – 800.00
   green ....$550.00 – 600.00
   tan ....$500.00 – 550.00

Page 124, Ivory II
1. Vase, 10" ....$75.00 – 95.00
2. Vase, 6", #259 ....$75.00 – 95.00

Page 125, Ivory II
Row 1:
Bowl vase, 6", #259 ....$75.00 – 95.00

Row 2:
1. Candelabrum, 5½", #1116, pr................$175.00 – 225.00
2. Bowl, 6" dia., #550.................................$40.00 – 50.00

Bleeding Heart
Row 1:
1. Vase, 4", #138, blue ....$125.00 – 150.00
   pink or green ....$100.00 – 125.00
2. Wall pocket, 8", #1287, blue..................$600.00 – 650.00
   pink or green ....$500.00 – 550.00
3. Pitcher, #1323, blue ....$550.00 – 600.00
   pink or green ....$450.00 – 500.00
4. Ewer, 6", #963, blue ....$275.00 – 300.00
   pink or green ....$250.00 – 275.00

Row 2:
1. Basket, 10", #360, blue ....$375.00 – 425.00
   pink or green ....$325.00 – 375.00
2. Basket, 12", #361, blue ....$550.00 – 600.00
   pink or green ....$450.00 – 500.00
3. Ewer, 10", #972, blue...........................$650.00 – 750.00
   pink or green ....$550.00 – 600.00

Page 126, Gardenia
Row 1:
Jardiniere, 4", #600 ....$90.00 – 110.00

Row 2:
1. Cornucopia, 6", #621.............................$100.00 – 125.00
2. Basket, 8", #608 ....$225.00 – 275.00
3. Ewer, 6", #616....................................$125.00 – 150.00

Row 3:
1. Ewer, 10", #617 ....$250.00 – 300.00
2. Basket, 10", #609 ....$300.00 – 350.00
3. Double cornucopia, 8", #622 ....$150.00 – 175.00

Page 127, Bittersweet
Row 1:
1. Double bud vase, 6", #873 ....$125.00 – 150.00
2. Basket, 10", #810 ....$250.00 – 300.00
3. Vase, 5", #972 ....$100.00 – 125.00

Row 2:
1. Planter, 8" wide, #868 ....$100.00 – 125.00
2. Tea set, #871 ....$450.00 – 550.00

Row 3:
1. Basket, 6", #808 ....$175.00 – 225.00
2. Basket, 8", #809 ....$200.00 – 250.00
3. Vase, 8", #883 ....$150.00 – 175.00
4. Cornucopia, 8", #822 ....$125.00 – 150.00
5. Ewer, 8", #816 ....$250.00 – 300.00

Page 129, White Rose
Row 1:
1. Frog, #41 ....$95.00 – 120.00
2. Cornucopia, 6", #143 ....$100.00 – 125.00
3. Bowl, 4", #387 ....$100.00 – 125.00
4. Bowl, 3", # 653 ....$95.00 – 115.00

Row 2:
1. Cornucopia, 8", #144 ....$125.00 – 150.00
2. Basket, 10", #363 ....$225.00 – 275.00
3. Bowl, 4", #653 ....$115.00 – 140.00
4. Ewer, 10", #990 ....$275.00 – 325.00

Row 3:
1. Double cornucopia, 8", #145 ....$125.00 – 150.00
2. Tea set, #1 ....$400.00 – 500.00
3. Vase, 8", #147 ....$150.00 – 175.00

Row 4:
1. Basket, 12", #364 ....$275.00 – 325.00
2. Ewer, 15", #993 ....$450.00 – 500.00
3. Ewer, 6", #981 ....$125.00 – 150.00
4. Pitcher, #1324 ....$225.00 – 250.00

Page 131, Water Lily
Row 1:
1. Jardiniere, 3", #663, rose with green ......$125.00 – 150.00
   blue ....$100.00 – 125.00
   brown ....$85.00 – 100.00
2. Ewer, 6", #10, rose with green ....$200.00 – 225.00
   blue ....$175.00 – 200.00
   brown ....$150.00 – 175.00
3. Vase, 6", #73, rose with green ....$175.00 – 200.00
   blue ....$150.00 – 175.00
   brown ....$125.00 – 150.00
4. Cornucopia, 6", #177, rose with green ...$175.00 – 200.00
   blue ....$150.00 – 175.00
   brown ....$125.00 – 150.00

Row 2:
1. Ewer, 10", #11, rose with green ....$350.00 – 400.00
   blue ....$325.00 – 350.00
   brown ....$300.00 – 325.00
2. Cookie jar, 10", #1, rose with green........$700.00 – 800.00
   blue ....$600.00 – 700.00
   brown ....$550.00 – 650.00
3. Basket, 10", #381, rose with green ....$375.00 – 400.00
   blue ....$350.00 – 375.00
   brown ....$325.00 – 350.00
4. Vase, 10", #80, rose with green ....$350.00 – 400.00
   blue ....$325.00 – 350.00
   brown ....$300.00 – 325.00

Row 3:
1. Vase, 7", #75, rose with green ....$125.00 – 150.00
   blue ....$110.00 – 130.00
   brown ....$95.00 – 110.00
2. Cornucopia, 8", #178, rose with green...$195.00 – 225.00
   blue ....$175.00 – 195.00
   brown ....$150.00 – 175.00
3. Vase, 6", #72, rose with green ....$100.00 – 125.00
   blue ....$85.00 – 100.00
   brown ....$75.00 – 95.00
4. Basket, 8", #380, rose with green ....$200.00 – 250.00
   blue ....$175.00 – 200.00
   brown ....$150.00 – 175.00

Row 4:
1. Vase, 12", #81, rose with green ....$425.00 – 475.00
   blue ....$275.00 – 425.00
   brown ....$350.00 – 400.00
2. Basket, 12", #382, rose with green ....$525.00 – 575.00
   blue ....$475.00 – 525.00
   brown ....$450.00 – 500.00
3. Ewer, 15", #12, rose with green...........$900.00 – 1,000.00
   blue ....$800.00 – 900.00
   brown ....$700.00 – 800.00

Page 133, Zephyr Lily
Row 1:
1. Jardiniere, 4", #671, blue ....$150.00 – 175.00
   brown ....$125.00 – 150.00
   green ....$100.00 – 125.00
2. Console boat, 10", #475, blue ....$250.00 – 275.00
   brown ....$225.00 – 250.00
   green ....$200.00 – 225.00
3. Center bowl, 8", #474, blue ....$150.00 – 175.00
   brown ....$125.00 – 150.00
   green ....$100.00 – 125.00

Row 2:
1. Basket, 7", #393, blue ....$175.00 – 200.00
   brown ....$150.00 – 175.00
   green ....$125.00 – 150.00
2. Cookie Jar, 10", #5, blue ....$750.00 – 850.00
   brown ....$600.00 – 675.00
   green ....$500.00 – 550.00
3. Ashtray, #29, blue ....$125.00 – 150.00
   brown ....$110.00 – 125.00
   green ....$95.00 – 110.00
4. Vase, 10", #138, blue ....$250.00 – 275.00

brown ....$225.00 – 250.00
green ....$200.00 – 225.00

Row 3:
1. Basket, 8", #394, blue ....$275.00 – 300.00
    brown ....$250.00 – 275.00
    green ....$225.00 – 250.00
2. Tea set, #7, blue.....................$550.00 – 600.00
    brown ....$450.00 – 525.00
    green ....$400.00 – 450.00
3. Cornucopia, 6", #203, blue....$150.00 – 175.00
    brown ....$125.00 – 150.00
    green ....$100.00 – 125.00

Row 4:
1. Basket, 10", #395, blue ....$375.00 – 400.00
    brown ....$325.00 – 350.00
    green ....$300.00 – 325.00
2. Vase, 7", #131, blue...............$175.00 – 200.00
    brown ....$150.00 – 175.00
    green ....$125.00 – 150.00
3. Ewer, 15", #24, blue...............$750.00 – 850.00
    brown ....$600.00 – 675.00
    green ....$500.00 – 550.00
4. Ewer, 10", #23, blue...............$375.00 – 400.00
    brown ....$350.00 – 375.00
    green ....$325.00 – 350.00
5. Vase, 10", #137, blue.............$325.00 – 350.00
    brown ....$300.00 – 325.00
    green ....$275.00 – 300.00

Page 135, Peony
Row 1:
1. Bowl, 3", #661 ....$95.00 – 125.00
2. Vase, 6", #168........................$110.00 – 135.00
3. Bowl, 4", #427 ....$100.00 – 125.00

Row 2:
1. Double cornucopia, #172 ....$125.00 – 150.00
2. Basket, 10", #378 ....$175.00 – 225.00
3. Basket, 7", #376 ....$125.00 – 150.00

Row 3:
1. Ewer, 6", #7 ....$100.00 – 125.00
2. Tea set, #3.............................$400.00 – 450.00
3. Bowl, 4", #661 ....$100.00 – 125.00

Row 4:
1. Vase, 4", #57 ....$75.00 – 85.00
2. Ewer, 10", #8 ....$200.00 – 225.00
3. Ewer, 10", #8 ....$200.00 – 225.00
4. Wall pocket, 8", #1293...........$250.00 – 300.00

Page 137, Magnolia
Row 1:
1. Planter, 8" wide, #389............$110.00 – 135.00
2. Double bud vase, 4½", #186 ....$100.00 – 125.00
3. Vase, 4", #86 ....$65.00 – 75.00
4. Bowl, 3", #665 ....$65.00 – 75.00

Row 2:
1. Ewer, 6", #13..........................$110.00 – 135.00

2. Mug, 3", #3 ....$125.00 – 150.00
3. Cider pitcher, 7", #1327 ....$300.00 – 350.00
4. Mug, 3", #3 ....$125.00 – 150.00
5. Basket, 8", #384 ....$150.00 – 200.00

Row 3:
1. Basket, 7", #383 ....$125.00 – 150.00
2. Tea set, #4.............................$400.00 – 450.00

Row 4:
1. Basket, 10", #385 ....$200.00 – 250.00
2. Ewer, 15", #15........................$350.00 – 400.00
3. Cookie jar, 10", #2 .... $450.00 – 550.00

Page 138, Columbine
Row 1:
1. Ewer, 7", #18, pink ....$275.00 – 300.00
    blue or tan ....$225.00 – 250.00
2. Bowl, 6", #401, pink................$150.00 – 175.00
    blue or tan ....$125.00 – 150.00
3. Basket, 7", #365, pink............$275.00 – 300.00
    blue or tan ....$225.00 – 250.00
4. Ewer, 7", #18, pink ....$275.00 – 300.00
    blue or tan ....$225.00 – 250.00

Row 2:
1. Basket, 10", #367, pink...........$350.00 – 400.00
    blue or tan ....$300.00 – 350.00
2. Bowl, 3", #655, pink................$150.00 – 175.00
    blue or tan ....$100.00 – 125.00
3. Basket, 12", #368, pink..........$450.00 – 500.00
    blue or tan ....$400.00 – 450.00
4. Vase, 8", #20, pink ....$250.00 – 300.00
    blue or tan ....$200.00 – 225.00

Page 139, Foxglove
Row 1:
1. Vase, 4", #42, green with pink ....$95.00 – 110.00
    blue ....$80.00 – 90.00
    pink ....$70.00 – 80.00
2. Vase, 3", #659, green with pink ....$85.00 – 95.00
    blue ....$75.00 – 85.00
    pink ....$65.00 – 75.00
3. Basket, 8", #373, green with pink.........$300.00 – 350.00
    blue ....$250.00 – 275.00
    pink ....$225.00 – 250.00
4. Conch shell, 6", #426, green with pink...$225.00 – 250.00
    blue ....$200.00 – 225.00
    pink ....$175.00 – 200.00
5. Double bud vase, 4½", #160,
    green w/pink ....$200.00 – 225.00
    blue ....$175.00 – 200.00
    pink ....$150.00 – 175.00

Row 2:
1. Ewer, 6½", #4, green with pink ....$275.00 – 300.00
    blue ....$250.00 – 275.00
    pink ....$225.00 – 250.00
2. Cornucopia, 8", #164, green with pink...$175.00 – 200.00
    blue ....$150.00 – 175.00
    pink ....$140.00 – 160.00

3. Candle holders, 4½", #1150,
    green with pink ....$225.00 – 250.00
    blue ....$200.00 – 225.00
    pink ....$175.00 – 200.00
4. Ewer, 15", #6, green with pink ....$850.00 – 950.00
    blue ....$750.00 – 850.00
    pink ....$700.00 – 800.00
5. Ewer, 10", #5, green with pink ....$450.00 – 500.00
    blue ....$400.00 – 450.00
    pink ....$375.00 – 400.00

Page 141, Freesia
Row 1:
1. Ewer, 6", #19, green.............................$275.00 – 325.00
    blue ....$250.00 – 275.00
    tangerine ....$225.00 – 250.00
2. Flowerpot, 5", #670, green ....$150.00 – 175.00
    blue ....$125.00 – 150.00
    tangerine ....$110.00 – 135.00
3. Bookends, pr., #15, green ....$375.00 – 425.00
    blue ....$375.00 – 400.00
    tangerine ....$350.00 – 375.00

Row 2:
1. Basket, 8", #391, green ....$300.00 – 350.00
    blue ....$275.00 – 300.00
    tangerine ....$250.00 – 275.00
2. Pitcher, 10", #20, green ....$375.00 – 400.00
    blue ....$350.00 – 375.00
    tangerine ....$325.00 – 350.00
3. Basket, 10", #392, green ....$425.00 – 475.00
    blue ....$400.00 – 425.00
    tangerine ....$375.00 – 400.00
4. Cornucopia, 8", #198, green....................$175.00 – 200.00
    blue ....$150.00 – 175.00
    tangerine ....$125.00 – 150.00

Row 3:
1. Vase, 8", #122, green..........................$250.00 – 275.00
    blue ....$225.00 – 250.00
    tangerine ....$200.00 – 225.00
2. Tea set, #6, green.............................$500.00 – 550.00
    blue ....$450.00 – 500.00
    tangerine ....$400.00 – 450.00
3. Vase, 7", #120, green..........................$200.00 – 225.00
    blue ....$175.00 – 200.00
    tangerine ....$160.00 – 170.00

Row 4:
1. Cookie jar, 10", #4, green ....$550.00 – 650.00
    blue ....$500.00 – 600.00
    tangerine ....$450.00 – 550.00
2. Ewer, 15", #21, green..........................$850.00 – 950.00
    blue ....$750.00 – 850.00
    tangerine ....$650.00 – 750.00
3. Vase, 8", #196, green..........................$275.00 – 300.00
    blue ....$250.00 – 275.00
    tangerine ....$225.00 – 250.00
4. Candle holders, 4½", #1161, pr., green..$200.00 – 225.00
    blue ....$175.00 – 200.00
    tangerine ....$160.00 – 180.00
5. Bud vase, 7", #195, green ....$175.00 – 200.00

blue ....$150.00 – 175.00
tangerine ....$135.00 – 160.00

Page 143, Clematis
Row 1:
1. Bowl, 4", #445, blue..............................$75.00 – 100.00
    green or brown.................................$60.00 – 75.00
2. Double bud vase, 5", #194, blue ....$125.00 – 150.00
    green or brown.................................$100.00 – 110.00
3. Cornucopia, 6", #190, blue....................$100.00 – 125.00
    green or brown.................................$90.00 – 110.00
4. Candle holders, 4½", #1159, pr., blue ....$150.00 – 175.00
    green or brown.................................$110.00 – 130.00

Row 2:
1. Basket, 8", #388, blue ....$250.00 – 275.00
    green or brown.................................$200.00 – 225.00
2. Bud vase, 7", #187, blue ....$150.00 – 175.00
    green or brown.................................$125.00 – 150.00
3. Ewer, 10", #17, blue...........................$250.00 – 275.00
    green or brown.................................$200.00 – 225.00
4. Basket, 7", #387, blue.........................$225.00 – 250.00
    green or brown.................................$175.00 – 200.00
5. Ewer, 6", #16, blue............................$175.00 – 200.00
    green or brown.................................$150.00 – 160.00

Row 3:
1. Vase, 8", #108, blue...........................$150.00 – 175.00
    green or brown.................................$120.00 – 140.00
2. Tea set, #5, blue..............................$450.00 – 500.00
    green or brown.................................$375.00 – 425.00
3. Vase, 6", #188, blue...........................$125.00 – 150.00
    green or brown.................................$100.00 – 110.00

Row 4:
1. Cookie jar, 10", #3, blue.......................$500.00 – 550.00
    green or brown.................................$400.00 – 450.00
2. Wall pocket, 8", #1295, blue.................$225.00 – 250.00
    green or brown.................................$200.00 – 225.00
3. Ewer, 15", #18, blue...........................$450.00 – 500.00
    green or brown.................................$400.00 – 450.00
4. Basket, 10", #389, blue ....$300.00 – 325.00
    green or brown.................................$250.00 – 275.00

Page 145, Apple Blossom
Row 1:
1. Cornucopia, 6", #321, blue....................$150.00 – 175.00
    pink or green..................................$125.00 – 150.00
2. Hanging basket, #361, blue....................$350.00 – 400.00
    pink or green..................................$300.00 – 350.00
3. Vase, 6", #381, blue...........................$150.00 – 175.00
    pink or green..................................$125.00 – 150.00

Row 2:
1. Tea set, #371, blue............................$650.00 – 750.00
    pink or green..................................$550.00 – 650.00
2. Basket, 8", #309, blue ....$325.00 – 375.00
    pink or green..................................$275.00 – 325.00

Row 3:
1. Ewer, 8", #316, blue...........................$275.00 – 325.00

pink or green ....$225.00 – 275.00
2. Vase, 7", #382, blue ....$175.00 – 200.00
   pink or green ....$150.00 – 175.00
3. Basket, 10", #310, blue ....$425.00 – 475.00
   pink or green ....$375.00 – 425.00
4. Bud vase, 7", #379, blue ....$175.00 – 200.00
   pink or green ....$150.00 – 175.00

Row 4:
1. Vase, 9", #387, blue ....$325.00 – 375.00
   pink or green ....$275.00 – 325.00
2. Ewer, 15, #318, blue ....$900.00 – 1,000.00
   pink or green ....$800.00 – 900.00
3. Basket, 12", #311, blue ....$525.00 – 575.00
   pink or green ....$450.00 – 500.00

Page 147, Bushberry
Row 1:
1. Bowl, 4", #411, blue..........................$150.00 – 175.00
   green ....$125.00 – 150.00
   orange ....$100.00 – 125.00
2. Basket, 6½", #369, blue ....$300.00 – 325.00
   green ....$250.00 – 275.00
   orange ....$200.00 – 225.00
3. Cornucopia, 6", #153, blue.................$150.00 – 175.00
   green ....$125.00 – 150.00
   orange ....$100.00 – 125.00
4. Vase, 6", #29, blue............................$150.00 – 175.00
   green ....$125.00 – 150.00
   orange ....$100.00 – 125.00
5. Jardiniere, 3", #657, blue...................$125.00 – 150.00
   green ....$100.00 – 125.00
   orange ....$80.00 – 90.00

Row 2:
1. Ewer, 6", #1, blue..............................$175.00 – 200.00
   green ....$150.00 – 175.00
   orange ....$125.00 – 150.00
2. Cornucopia, #3, blue ....$200.00 – 225.00
   green ....$175.00 – 200.00
   orange ....$150.00 – 175.00
3. Wall pocket, 8", #1291, blue...............$550.00 – 600.00
   green ....$450.00 – 500.00
   orange ....$400.00 – 450.00
4. Basket, 8", #370, blue ....$300.00 – 350.00
   green ....$250.00 – 300.00
   orange ....$200.00 – 250.00

Row 3:
   Tea set, #2, blue.................................$600.00 – 700.00
   green ....$500.00 – 600.00
   orange ....$450.00 – 500.00

Row 4:
1. Ewer, 10", #2, blue.............................$400.00 – 450.00
   green ....$350.00 – 400.00
   orange ....$300.00 – 350.00
2. Basket, 12", #372, blue ....$450.00 – 500.00
   green ....$400.00 – 450.00
   orange ....$350.00 – 400.00
3. Cornucopia, 8", #154, blue..................$175.00 – 200.00

green ....$150.00 – 175.00
orange ....$125.00 – 150.00

Page 149, Snowberry
Row 1:
1. Ashtray, #1AT, blue or pink ....$150.00 – 175.00
   green ....$125.00 – 150.00
2. Center bowl, 10" wide, #1BL1,
   blue or pink ....$150.00 – 175.00
   green ....$125.00 – 150.00
3. Ewer, 6", #1TK, blue or pink ....$125.00 – 150.00
   green ....$100.00 – 125.00

Row 2:
1. Basket, 7", #1BK, blue or pink ....$150.00 – 175.00
   green ....$125.00 – 150.00
2. Cornucopia, 6", #1CC, blue or pink ......$100.00 – 125.00
   green ....$90.00 – 110.00
3. Basket, 8", #1BK, blue or pink ....$250.00 – 275.00
   green ....$225.00 – 250.00
4. Rose bowl, 5", #1RB, blue or pink ....$150.00 – 175.00
   green ....$125.00 – 150.00

Row 3:
1. Ewer, 6", #1TK, blue or pink ....$150.00 – 175.00
   green ....$125.00 – 150.00
2. Tea set, #1TP, #1S, #1C, blue or pink.....$450.00 – 500.00
   green ....$400.00 – 450.00
3. Bud vase, 7", #1BV, blue or pink ....$100.00 – 120.00
   green ....$85.00 – 95.00

Row 4:
1. Basket, 8", #1BK, blue or pink ....$250.00 – 275.00
   green ....$225.00 – 250.00
2. Ewer, 10", #1TK, blue or pink ....$300.00 – 350.00
   green ....$250.00 – 275.00
3. Candle holders, #1CS1, pr.,
   blue or pink ....$125.00 – 150.00
   green ....$100.00 – 125.00
4. Basket, 10", #1BK, blue or pink ....$300.00 – 350.00
   green ....$275.00 – 300.00

Page 150, Mayfair
Center:
1. Bowl, 4", #1110 ....$50.00 – 75.00
2. Pitcher, 8", #1105..............................$150.00 – 175.00
3. Tankard, 12", #1107 ....$175.00 – 200.00
4. Planter, 8", #1113................................$60.00 – 75.00

Page 151, Mock Orange
Row 1:
1. Jardiniere, 4", #900............................$75.00 – 100.00
2. Basket, 6", #908 ....$125.00 – 150.00
3. Ewer, 6", #916...................................$125.00 – 150.00

Row 2:
1. Planter, 7", #981................................$150.00 – 175.00

Row 3:
1. Basket, 8", #909, each.........................$250.00 – 300.00

Page 152, Burmese
1. Candle holder/bookends, pr.
   White, #82 – B ....$225.00 – 250.00
   Black, #70 – B...........................$250.00 – 275.00
2. Candlestick, #75 – B, pr......................... $50.00 – 60.00

Royal Capri
   Bowl, 7", #GR-526 ....$300.00 – 350.00

Page 153, Ming Tree
Row 1:
1. Candle holders, #551, pr.......................$100.00 – 125.00
2. Basket, 8", #508 ....$125.00 – 150.00

Row 2:
1. Center bowl, 10" across, #528 ....$125.00 – 150.00

Row 3:
1. Vase, 8", #582....................................$100.00 – 125.00
2. Ewer, 10", #516.................................$150.00 – 175.00
3. Vase, 6", #581.....................................$75.00 – 85.00

Page 154, Lotus
1. Candle holders, 2½", #L5, pr. ....$125.00 – 150.00
2. Vase, 10", #L3....................................$300.00 – 350.00

Page 155, Pasadena
1. Planter, 7", #526...................................$50.00 – 60.00
2. Flowerpot, 4", #L36 ....$60.00 – 70.00
3. Bowl, 3", #L24 ....$60.00 – 75.00
4. Flowerpot, 4", #L36 ....$60.00 – 70.00

Florane II
1. Vase, 6", #80 ....$50.00 – 60.00
2. Vase, 7", #81 ....$75.00 – 85.00
3. Vase, 9", #82 ....$95.00 – 110.00
4. Bowl, 9", #61 ....$85.00 – 95.00

Page 157, Elsie the Cow
1. Mug, #B1..$250.00 – 300.00
2. Plate, 7½", #B2 ....$300.00 – 350.00
3. Bowl, #B3...$350.00 – 400.00

Capri
Row 1:
1. Vase, 9", #582....................................$100.00 – 125.00
2. Leaf Tray, 15", #532 ....$65.00 – 75.00
3. Boat-shape dish, 7", #555 ....$40.00 – 50.00

Row 2:
1. Ming Tree Conch shell, 7½", #563..........$100.00 – 125.00
2. Shell ....$50.00 – 60.00
3. Bowl, 9", #529 ....$30.00 – 40.00

Unnamed Line
Row 2:
4. Teapot, #14-P....................................$125.00 – 150.00

Page 159, Silhouette
Row 1:
1. Candle holders, 3", #751, pr. ....$100.00 – 125.00
2. Planter, 14" long, #731...........................$125.00 – 150.00

Row 2:
1. Planter vase, 5", #756..............................$85.00 – 95.00
2. Ewer, 6", #716.......................................$100.00 – 125.00
3. Ewer, 10", #717.....................................$175.00 – 200.00
4. Basket, 6", #708.....................................$150.00 – 175.00
5. Vase, 7", #782...$85.00 – 95.00

Row 3:
1. Cornucopia, 8", #721...............................$85.00 – 95.00
2. Fan vase, 7", #783.................................$400.00 – 450.00
3. Ashtray, #799...$75.00 – 85.00
4. Basket, 8", #709.....................................$175.00 – 200.00

Row 4:
1. Basket, 10", #710...................................$250.00 – 300.00
2. Cigarette box, #740 ....$150.00 – 175.00
3. Vase, 8", #763.......................................$500.00 – 650.00
4. Vase, 9", #785.......................................$150.00 – 175.00
5. Wall pocket, 8", #766.............................$225.00 – 275.00

Page 161, Wincraft
Row 1:
1. Planter set, 6", #1050 and #1051 ....$175.00 – 225.00
2. Tea set, #271.......................................$225.00 – 250.00

Row 2:
1. Basket, 12", #209 ....$175.00 – 200.00
2. Candle holders, #2CS, pr........................$75.00 – 85.00
3. Artwood Circle vase, 8", #1053 ....$150.00 – 175.00
4. Ewer, 8", #216.....................................$125.00 – 150.00

Row 3:
1. Planter, 10", #231.................................$125.00 – 150.00
2. Cornucopia, 8", #222.............................$125.00 – 150.00
3. Ewer, 6", #217.......................................$95.00 – 105.00
4. Basket, 8", #208 ....$150.00 – 175.00

Row 4:
1. Vase, 8", #282......................................$150.00 – 175.00
2. Vase, 10", #284....................................$225.00 – 250.00
3. Vase, 10", #290.................................$900.00 – 1,000.00
4. Vase, 10", #285....................................$200.00 – 250.00
5. Vase, 6", #272.......................................$95.00 – 105.00

Page 162, Raymor
1. Bean pot, #195 ....$50.00 – 60.00
2. Swinging coffeepot, #176 ....$450.00 – 500.00
3. Bean pot, #194 ....$60.00 – 70.00

Page 163, Raymor
Row 1:
1. Hot plate, #84-198 and casserole, #198 ....$75.00 – 85.00
2. Hot plate, #159 ....$35.00 – 40.00
3. Cup and saucer, #151.............................$25.00 – 30.00

Row 2:
1. Tea set (Sugar, #157, Creamer, #158).....$250.00 – 300.00

Row 3:
1. Salad plate, #154 ....$15.00 – 20.00
2. Dinner plate, #152......................................$20.00 – 30.00
3. Luncheon plate, #153 ....$15.00 – 20.00

Page 165, Jardinieres and pedestals, umbrella stands
Plate 140
33" Blackberry set (12" jardiniere) ....$5,000.00 – 6,000.00
29" Blackberry set (10" jardiniere) ....$3,500.00 – 4,500.00
29" Donatello set (10" jardiniere) .....$1,000.00 – 1,100.00
30" Pine Cone set (10"
jardiniere), blue ....$4,500.00 – 5,500.00
brown ....$3,000.00 – 3,500.00
green ....$2,500.00 – 3,000.00
33½" Pine Cone set (8"
jardiniere), blue...............................$6,000.00 – 7,000.00
brown ....$4,500.00 – 5,500.00
green ....$3,500.00 – 4,500.00
24" Pine Cone set (8" jardiniere),
blue ....$3,000.00 – 4,000.00
brown ....$2,000.00 – 2,500.00
green ....$1,750.00 – 2,250.00
32" Magnolia set (10" jardiniere), with handles,
blue ....$2,000.00 – 2,500.00
green ....$1,750.00 – 2,000.00
brown ....$1,500.00 – 1,750.00
without handles, blue.......................$1,750.00 – 2,000.00
without handles, green.....................$1,500.00 – 1,750.00
without handles, brown.....................$1,250.00 – 1,500.00
24" Magnolia set (8" jardiniere), with handles
blue ....$1,250.00 – 1,500.00
green $1,100.00– 1,250.00
brown ....$900.00 – 1,150.00
without handles, blue.......................$1,100.00 – 1,250.00
without handles, green.....................$950.00 – 1,100.00
without handles, brown.........................$800.00 – 950.00

Plate 141
Mostique umbrella stand ....$800.00 – 900.00
Mostique jardiniere and pedestal,
28½" ....$1,250.00 – 1,500.00
Fuchsia jardiniere and pedestal, 31" set (10" jardiniere)
blue ....$4,500.00 – 5,500.00
green ....$3,000.00 – 3,500.00
brown/tan..$2,500.00 – 3,000.00
Fuchsia jardiniere and pedestal, 24" set (8" jardiniere)
blue ....$2,500.00 – 3,000.00
green ....$1,750.00 – 2,000.00
brown/tan..$1,500.00 – 1,750.00
Freesia jardiniere and pedestal, 24" set (8" jardiniere)
blue ....$1,250.00 – 1,500.00
green ....$1,000.00 – 1,200.00
tangerine ....$900.00 – 1,100.00

Page 166, Miscellaneous
Factory lamp ....$850.00 – 950.00

Page 167, Miscellaneous
Moderne trial glaze vase, 8", #796 ....$600.00 – 700.00
Crystal Green vase, 8", #942 ....$150.00 – 200.00
Capri basket, 10", #C-1012 ....$100.00 – 150.00
Vista basket, 8" ....$800.00 – 900.00

Page 168, Umbrella stands and sand jars
Imperial I umbrella stand ....$900.00 – 1,000.00
Florentine umbrella stand ....$1,000.00 – 1,250.00
Pine Cone umbrella stand, green .....$1,750.00 – 2,250.00
brown ....$2,500.00 – 3,000.00
blue ....$3,000.00 – 3,500.00
Florentine II sand jar ....$900.00 – 1,000.00

PRICE GUIDE — VOLUME II, REVISED EDITION

Page 3, Luffa
    Jardiniere and pedestal, 30" ....$3,000.00 – 3,500.00

Page 4, Wincraft
    Dealer sign, 4½" x 8" ....$5,000.00 – 6,000.00

Page 6, Woodland vase, 19" ....$3,500.00 – 4,500.00

Page 10, Decorated Matt
    Umbrella stand, 20", #724 ....$5,000.00 – 6,000.00

Page 18, Rozane
    1. Vase, 12", #818 ....$600.00 – 700.00
    2. Vase, 7", #843 ....$350.00 – 450.00
    3. Vase, 5", #874 ....$275.00 – 375.00

Row 1:
    1. Vase, 9½" ....$3,500.00 – 4,000.00
    2. Pillow vase, 8½" ....$2,000.00 – 2,500.00
    3. Vase, 8½" ....$3,000.00 – 3,500.00

Row 2:
    1. Pillow vase, 9", #882 ....$2,000.00 – 2,500.00
    2. Vase, 8" ....$2,000.00 – 2,500.00
    3. Pillow vase, 9" ....$2,500.00 – 3,000.00

Row 3:
    1. Vase, 13" ....$3,000.00 – 4,000.00
    2. Vase, 17", #931 ....$3,500.00 – 4,500.00
    3. Vase, 14" ....$3,500.00 – 4,500.00

Page 19, Rozane, 1900s
    1. Vase, 12" ....$700.00 – 750.00
    2. Three-sided vase, 8", #1213/188......$1,500.00 – 2,000.00
    3. Mug, 5" ....$800.00 – 1,000.00

Row 1:
    1. Vase, 5½", #872 ....$175.00 – 200.00
    2. Vase, 6½", #840/6......................$125.00 – 150.00
    3. Vase, 9" ....$150.00 – 175.00
    4. Vase, 8" ....$200.00 – 250.00
    5. Pillow vase, 5", #904/7 ....$150.00 – 175.00

Row 2:
    1. Ewer, 7½", #857/x...................$150.00 – 175.00
    2. Vase, 10" ....$175.00 – 200.00
    3. Vase, 13", #837/3......................$200.00 – 275.00
    4. Vase, 11", #902/3......................$250.00 – 275.00
    5. Ewer, 7½",#950 ....$150.00 – 175.00

Row 3:
    1. Vase, 10½", #5 ....$200.00 – 250.00
    2. Paperweight, 4½" ....$225.00 – 275.00
    3. Jardiniere, 9½" ....$150.00 – 200.00
    4. Vase, 11", #7 ....$300.00 – 350.00

Page 20, Rozane, 1900s
    Roseville sign, 3" x 8¼" ....$1,500.00 – 2,000.00

Row 1:
    1. Vase, 7¼" ....$200.00 – 250.00
    2. Tankard, 10½", #821 ....$400.00 – 500.00
    3. Candlestick, 9".........................$275.00 – 300.00
    4. Vase, 7½", #836 ....$175.00 – 225.00

Row 2:
    1. Vase, 8" ....$2,550.00 – 3,000.00
    2. Pillow vase, 9", #882 ....$2,000.00 – 2,500.00
    3. Vase, 7½" ....$300.00 – 350.00

Row 3:
    1. Vase, 14", #891 ....$3,500.00 – 4,500.00
    2. Vase, 15" ....$1,500.00 – 2,000.00
    3. Vase, 14", #891 ....$2,500.00 – 3,500.00

Page 21, Rozane
Row 1:
    1. Letter holder, 3½" ....$250.00 – 300.00
    2. Mug, 4½", #856 ....$350.00 – 400.00
    3. Bud vase, 6½", #875 ....$250.00 – 300.00
    4. Bud vase, 6½", #915 ....$150.00 – 175.00
    5. Mug, 5" ....$200.00 – 250.00
    6. Mug, 4½", #856 ....$150.00 – 175.00

Row 2:
    1. Vase, 10" ....$700.00 – 800.00
    2. Vase, 11" ....$550.00 – 650.00
    3. Ewer, 10½" ....$350.00 – 450.00

Row 3:
    1. Vase, 13" ....$400.00 – 450.00
    2. Tankard, 14" ....$300.00 – 350.00
    3. Vase, 18½", #865 ....$800.00 – 900.00
    4. Vase, 15" ....$600.00 – 700.00
    5. Vase, 10½" ....$500.00 – 600.00

Page 22, Rozane
Row 1:
    1. Bud vase, 7½", #841/3 ....$150.00 – 200.00
    2. Bud vase, 8" ....$150.00 – 200.00
    3. Pillow vase, 7" ....$300.00 – 350.00
    4. Vase, 8½" ....$200.00 – 250.00
    5. Vase, 6½" ....$150.00 – 200.00

Row 2:
    1. Vase, 8½" ....$200.00 – 250.00
    2. Vase, 10½" ....$300.00 – 350.00
    3. Pillow vase, 8½" ....$350.00 – 400.00
    4. Vase, 11" ....$250.00 – 300.00
    5. Vase, 10½" ....$200.00 – 250.00

Row 3:
    1. Vase, 14" ....$450.00 – 500.00
    2. Ewer, 16", #858........................$1,000.00 – 1,250.00
    3. Tankard, 15½" ....$1,000.00 – 1,250.00
    4. Mug, 6" ....$300.00 – 350.00

Page 23, Rozane
Row 1:
    1. Vase, 8" ....$300.00 – 350.00
    2. Vase, 9½" ....$200.00 – 250.00
    3. Vase, 11½", #833/3 ....$250.00 – 300.00
    4. Chocolate pot, 9½", #936/7 ....$500.00 – 600.00

Row 2:
    1. Mug, 4", #856/6 ....$150.00 – 175.00
    2. Mug, 6" ....$200.00 – 250.00
    3. Pillow vase, 7" ....$300.00 – 350.00
    4. Mug, 4", #856/2 ....$150.00 – 175.00

Row 3:
    1. Tankard, 16" ....$550.00 – 650.00
    2. Vase, 16" ....$500.00 – 600.00
    3. Tankard, 15½" ....$450.00 – 500.00

Page 24, Vase Assortment #24
    1. Vase, 8", #107 ....$300.00 – 325.00
    2. Vase, 9", #102 ....$325.00 – 375.00
    3. Vase, 9", #110 ....$325.00 – 375.00
    4. Vase, 8", #108 ....$325.00 – 375.00
    5. Vase, 7", #109 ....$275.00 – 325.00

Azurean
Row 1:
    1. Vase, 9" ....$2,500.00 – 3,000.00

Row 2:
    1. Candlestick, 9" ....$550.00 – 650.00
    2. Vase, 7½", #4 ....$550.00 – 650.00
    3. Mug, #4 ....$400.00 – 450.00

Row 3:
    1. Vase, 14" ....$2,000.00 – 2,500.00
    2. Vase, 18", #865 ....$2,000.00 – 2,250.00
    3. Vase, 15½", #822/7 ....$1,750.00 – 2,250.00

Page 25, Rozane Light
    1. Home Art jardiniere, 5" ....$175.00 – 200.00
    2. Vase, 11½" ....$750.00 – 850.00
    3. Vase, 15" ....$3,000.00 – 3,500.00

Row 1:
    1. Bowl, 3" ....$250.00 – 300.00
    2. Vase, 4" ....$200.00 – 250.00
    3. Home Art jardiniere, 5" ....$175.00 – 200.00
    4. Mug, 5" ....$350.00 – 400.00

Row 2:
    1. Pillow vase, 6½" ....$400.00 – 500.00
    2. Vase, 8½" ....$4,000.00 – 5,000.00
    3. Pillow vase, 7" ....$450.00 – 550.00

Row 3:
    1. Vase, 6½" ....$350.00 – 400.00
    2. Vase, 13" ....$550.00 – 650.00
    3. Vase, 18" ....$1,500.00 – 1,750.00
    4. Vase, 14" ....$3,000.00 – 3,500.00
    5. Vase, 8½" ....$500.00 – 600.00

Page 26, Rozane Light
Row 1:
    1. Sugar Bowl, 4½" ....$250.00 – 300.00
    2. Teapot, 8", #60 ....$4,000.00 – 5,000.00
    3. Mug, 5" ....$300.00 – 350.00

Row 2:
    1. Vase, 8" ....$400.00 – 500.00
    2. Vase, 8" ....$400.00 – 500.00
    3. Vase, 10" ....$600.00 – 700.00
    4. Vase, 10" ....$650.00 – 750.00
    5. Vase, 8½" ....$450.00 – 550.00

Row 3:
    1. Tankard, 11" ....$700.00 – 800.00
    2. Vase, 11" ....$650.00 – 750.00
    3. Tankard, 16" ....$1,500.00 – 1,750.00
    4. Vase, 10½" ....$650.00 – 750.00
    5. Tankard, 10" ....$1,200.00 – 1,400.00

Page 28, Mara
    1. Bowl, 4" ....$2,000.00 – 2,500.00
    2. Vase, 13" ....$1,500.00 – 1,750.00

    1. Vase, 5½" ....$2,000.00 – 2,500.00
    2. Vase, 5½", #13 ....$1,750.00 – 2,250.00

Page 29, Olympic
Row 1:
    1. Pitcher, 7" ....$2,500.00 – 3,000.00
    2. Pitcher, 7" ....$2,500.00 – 3,000.00

Row 2:
    1. Vase, 14½" ....$7,500.00 – 8,500.00
    2. Vase, 20" ....$8,500.00 – 9,500.00

Page 30, Mongol
Row 1:
    1. Mug, 6" ....$700.00 – 850.00
    2. Vase, 5" ....$500.00 – 600.00

Row 2:
    1. Vase, 10½", #C-16 ....$3,000.00 – 3,500.00
    2. Vase, 14" ....$2,000.00 – 2,500.00
    3. Vase, 16" ....$2,000.00 – 2,500.00

Page 31, Mongol
    1. Vase, 8" ....$1,000.00 – 1,250.00
    2. Vase, 10½" ....$1,250.00 – 2,500.00

    1. Vase, 7", #120 ....$3,000.00 – 4,000.00
    2. Vase, 2½" ....$400.00 – 500.00

Page 32
    1. Vase, 6" ....$2,000.00 – 2,500.00
    2. Pitcher, 7½" ....$2,500.00 – 3,000.00
    3. Vase, 11" ....$4,500.00 – 5,000.00
    Paper collectibles ....$20.00 – 35.00

Page 33, Woodland
Row 1:
    1. Vase, 6" ....$400.00 – 450.00
    2. Vase, 6½" ....$550.00 – 650.00
    3. Vase, 6½' ....$450.00 – 550.00
    4. Vase, 7" ....$450.00 – 550.00

Row 2:
    1. Vase, 9" ....$800.00 – 900.00
    2. Vase, 9" ....$700.00 – 800.00
    3. Vase, 11" ....$700.00 – 800.00
    4. Vase, 11½" ....$700.00 – 800.00
    5. Vase, 10" ....$800.00 – 900.00
    6. Vase, 9" ....$600.00 – 700.00

Row 3:
    1. Vase, 13" ....$3,000.00 – 3,500.00
    2. Vase, 19" ....$4,500.00 – 5,500.00
    3. Vase, 15½" ....$2,500.00 – 3,000.00
    4. Vase, 15" ....$3,000.00 – 3,500.00

Page 34, Fudji
    1. Vase, 9" ....$2,500.00 – 3,000.00
    2. Vase, 10½" ....$3,500.00 – 4,500.00
    3. Vase, 10" ....$3,000.00 – 3,500.00

Fudjiyama
    1. Vase, 15" ....$1,750.00 – 2,000.00
    2. Jardiniere, 9" ....$2,500.00 – 3,000.00
    3. Vase, 11" ....$1,500.00 – 1,750.00
    4. Vase, 9" ....$1,500.00 – 1,750.00
    Paper collectibles ....$20.00 – 35.00

Page 35, Della Robbia
Row 1:
    1. Teapot, 6" ....$2,500.00 – 3,000.00
    2. Teapot, 5½" ....$2,500.00 – 3,000.00
    3. Teapot, 6" ....$3,000.00 – 3,500.00

Row 2:
    1. Mug, 4½" ....$1,250.00 – 1,500.00
    2. Pitcher, 8" ....$4,000.00 – 5,000.00
    3. Mug, 4½" ....$750.00 – 800.00

Row 1:
    1. Tankard, 10½" ....$6,500.00 – 7,500.00
    2. Teapot, 6½" ....$3,000.00 – 3,500.00
    3. Tankard, 10½" ....$2,000.00 – 2,500.00

Row 2:
    1. Vase, 10" ....$6,000.00 – 7,000.00
    2. Vase, 11" ....$3,000.00 – 3,500.00
    3. Vase, 9" ....$2,500.00 – 3,000.00

Page 36, Della Robbia
Row 1:
    1. Vase, 8" ....$7,000.00 – 8,000.00
    2. Teapot, 8" ....$2,000.00 – 2,500.00
    3. Vase, 8½" ....$5,000.00 – 6,000.00

Row 2:
    1. Mug, 4" ....$750.00 – 850.00
    2. Jar, 8", without lid ....$3,000.00 – 3,500.00
       with lid...$6,000.00 – 7,000.00
    3. Vase, 9½" ....$2,500.00 – 3,000.00
    4. Bowl, 8" x 2½" ....$3,500.00 – 4,500.00
    5. Letter holder, 3½" ....$1,300.00 – 1,500.00

Row 3:
    1. Vase, 15" ....$8,000.00 – 9,000.00
    2. Vase, 14" ....$8,000.00 – 9,000.00
    3. Vase, 11½" ....$12,500.00 – 15,000.00
    4. Vase, 11½" ....$9,000.00 – 10,000.00

Plate 28:
    Vase, 19" ....$30,000.00 – 35,000.00

Plate 29:
    Vase, 12" ....$15,000.00 – 17,500.00

Plate 30:
    Vase, 8½" ....$8,500.00 – 9,500.00

Page 37, Crystalis
    1. Vase, 14" ....$3,500.00 – 4,000.00
    2. Pot, 3" ....$1,500.00 – 1,750.00

Page 38, Crystalis
    1. Candlestick, 9" ....$900.00 – 1,000.00
    2. Vase, 12½" ....$3,500.00 – 4,000.00
    3. Vase, 13" ....$1,750.00 – 2,250.00
    4. Vase, 11" ....$2,500.00 – 3,000.00
    5. Vase, 5½" ....$1,200.00 – 1,400.00

Various Early Lines
Row 1:
    1. Vase, 3½" ....$600.00 – 700.00
    2. Planter, 4" ....$400.00 – 500.00
    3. Vase, 7", #501 ....$400.00 – 500.00
    4. Vase, 5½" ....$600.00 – 700.00

Row 2:
    1. Vase, 11" ....$1,250.00 – 1,500.00
    2. Vase, 9" ....$2,000.00 – 2,500.00
    3. Vase, 8½" ....$800.00 – 900.00
    4. Weller vase
    5. Vase, 12" ....$1,250.00 – 1,500.00

Page 39, Blue Ware
    1. Mug, 6" ....$400.00 – 500.00
    2. Teapot, 8" ....$400.00 – 500.00
    3. Teapot, 7" ....$800.00 – 900.00
    4. Teapot, 4" ....$300.00 – 400.00

Special
    1. Mug, 5" ....$200.00 – 250.00
    2. Tankard, 12" ....$400.00 – 450.00
    3. Mug, 5" ....$175.00 – 225.00
    4. Tankard, 15½", #884 ....$550.00 – 600.00

1. Pillow vase, 9", #882 ....$4,000.00 – 5,000.00
2. Vase, 9" ....$350.00 – 450.00

Page 40, Decorated Art
Row 1:
    1. Jardiniere, 8" ....$300.00 – 350.00
    2. Vase, 12½", #20 ....$400.00 – 450.00
    3. Jardiniere, 6" ....$175.00 – 225.00

Row 2:
    1. Jardiniere, 10", #448 ....$500.00 – 600.00
    2. Vase, 16" ....$1,250.00 – 1,500.00

Chloron
    1. Vase, 6½" ....$450.00 – 500.00
    2. Vase, 12" ....$1,100.00 – 1,200.00
    3. Vase, 9" ....$800.00 – 900.00

Page 41, Egypto
    1. Pitcher vase, 11" ....$1,750.00 – 2,000.00
    2. Lamp base, 10" ....$3,500.00 – 4,000.00
    3. Vase, 6½" ....$700.00 – 750.00
    4. Pitcher, 7" ....$700.00 – 750.00
    5. Vase, 5½" ....$600.00 – 650.00

Matt Green
Row 1:
    1. Pot/liner, 3" ....$75.00 – 100.00
    2. Pot/liner, 3" ....$100.00 – 125.00
    3. Pot/liner, 4" ....$75.00 – 100.00
    4. Gate, 5" x 8" ....$125.00 – 150.00
    5. Pot/frog, 2½" ....$100.00 – 125.00

Row 2:
    1. Jardiniere, 6" ....$250.00 – 300.00
    2. Tobacco jar, 6" ....$300.00 – 350.00
    3. Planter/liner, 4" x 8" ....$450.00 – 500.00
    4. Jardiniere, 5½", #456 ....$250.00 – 300.00

Page 42, Chloron, Egypto, and Matt Green
Top:
    1. Matt Green, Hanging basket, 9" ....$150.00 – 200.00

Row 1:
    1. Matt Green, Planter/liner, 4", #510 ....$200.00 – 250.00
    2. Chloron, Candlestick, 4" ....$250.00 – 300.00
    3. Egypto, Creamer, 3½" ....$400.00 – 450.00
    4. Egypto, Bud vase, 5½" ....$450.00 – 500.00
    5. Chloron, Bowl, 3" ....$300.00 – 350.00

Row 2:
    1. Chloron, Jardiniere, 5½", #487 ....$400.00 – 450.00
    2. Chloron, Vase, 7" ....$900.00 – 1,000.00
    3. Chloron, Vase, 9" ....$1,000.00 – 1,250.00

Row 3:
    1. Egypto, Vase, 12½" ....$1,750.00 – 2,000.00
    2. Egypto, Pitcher, 12" ....$2,000.00 – 2,500.00
    3. Egypto, Circle jug, 11" ....$3,500.00 – 4,000.00
    4. Matt Green, Planter, 5½" ....$300.00 – 350.00

Page 43, Pauleo
    1. Vase, 19", #340 ....$1,250.00 – 1,500.00
    2. Bowl, 3" ....$800.00 – 1,000.00
    3. Vase, 19" ....$2,500.00 – 3,000.00

Row 1:
    1. Vase, 9" ....$700.00 – 800.00
    2. Vase, 12" ....$1,250.00 – 1,500.00
    3. Vase, 9" ....$700.00 – 800.00

Row 2:
    1. Vase, 18½" ....$2,500.00 – 3,000.00
    2. Vase, 19' ....$1,750.00 – 2,000.00
    3. Vase, 20½" ....$1,750.00 – 2,000.00

Page 45, Pauleo
Row 1:
    1. Vase, 17" ....$1,750.00 – 2,000.00
    2. Vase, 14" ....$1,750.00 – 2,000.00

Row 2:
    1. Vase, 17½" ....$1,500.00 – 1,750.00
    2. Vase, 19" ....$1,500.00 – 1,750.00
    3. Vase, 16½" ....$1,250.00 – 1,500.00

Page 46, Pauleo
Row 1:
    1. Vase, 16½" ....$2,000.00 – 2,500.00
    2. Vase, 14" ....$1,500.00 – 1,750.00
    3. Vase, 16½" ....$1,250.00 – 1,500.00

Row 2:
    1. Vase, 15½" ....$4,000.00 – 4,500.00
    2. Vase, 17" ....$3,000.00 – 3,500.00

Page 47, Cornelian, Colonial, Venetian, and Holland
Row 1:
    1. Cornelian Shaving mug, 4" ....$65.00 – 75.00
    2. Cornelian Mush bowl, 3" & Pitcher, 5½" ..$80.00 – 100.00
    3. Cornleian Toothbrush holder, 5" ....$60.00 – 70.00
    4. Cornelian Soap dish, 4" ....$75.00 – 85.00

Row 2:
    1. Colonial Soap dish, 4" ....$80.00 – 90.00
    2. Venetian Salesman's sample, #3 ....$70.00 – 80.00
    3. Cornelian Shaving mug, 4" ....$65.00 – 75.00
    4. Holland pitcher, 12" ....$400.00 – 500.00

Row 3:
    1. Cornelian Pitcher, 12" & Bowl, 15½" ......$350.00 – 450.00
    2. Colonial Combinet, 12" ....$300.00 – 350.00

Page 48, Cornelian
Row 1:
    1. Pitcher, 4" ....$50.00 – 60.00
    2. Pitcher, 5" ....$75.00 – 85.00
    3. Pitcher, 9" ....$125.00 – 150.00
    4. Pitcher, 5½" ....$75.00 – 85.00
    5. Pitcher, 5" ....$125.00 – 150.00

Row 2:
1. Pitcher, 6"..$125.00 – 150.00
2. Jardiniere, 7"..................................$95.00 – 110.00
3. Jardiniere, 6½", #119.......................$100.00 – 125.00

Colonial
1. Pitcher, 7½".....................................$100.00 – 125.00
2. Pitcher, 11".....................................$175.00 – 250.00
3. Bowl, 16"..$150.00 – 200.00
3. Toothbrush holder, 5"......................$85.00 – 95.00

Holland
1. Powder jar, 3".................................$100.00 – 125.00
2. Tankard, #2, 9½".............................$200.00 – 250.00
3. Pitcher, #1, 6½"..............................$200.00 – 250.00
4. Mug, 4"..$65.00 – 75.00

Page 49, Aztec
1. Vase, 9"..$400.00 – 500.00
2. Vase, 11"..$600.00 – 700.00
3. Vase, 11"..$600.00 – 700.00
4. Vase, 9"..$400.00 – 500.00
5. Vase, 8"..$400.00 – 500.00

1. Vase, 11½".......................................$500.00 – 600.00
2. Vase, 10½".......................................$400.00 – 500.00
3. Vase, 9½"...$400.00 – 500.00

Page 50, Crocus
1. Vase, 7"..$500.00 – 600.00
2. Vase, 9½"...$600.00 – 700.00
3. Vase, 9"..$600.00 – 700.00
4. Vase, 7"..$500.00 – 600.00

1. Vase, 9"..$600.00 – 700.00
2. Vase, 7"..$500.00 – 600.00
3. Vase, 6"..$500.00 – 600.00
4. Letter receiver, 3½".........................$400.00 – 500.00

Page 51, Early Pitchers
Row 1:
1. Osiris Utility pitcher, 6½".................$100.00 – 125.00
2. Osiris Pitcher, 8" ....$125.00 – 150.00

Row 2:
1. Pitcher, 6"......................................$175.00 – 225.00
2. Pitcher, 7½".....................................$400.00 – 500.00
3. Pitcher, 6"......................................$150.00 – 175.00

Row 3:
1. Pitcher, 9½".....................................$250.00 – 300.00
2. Pitcher, 8"......................................$450.00 – 500.00
3. Pitcher, 9½".....................................$200.00 – 250.00

Page 52, Early Pitchers
1. Pitcher, 9", #11..............................$300.00 – 350.00
2. Pitcher, 9", #141............................$300.00 – 350.00

Row 1:
1. Pitcher, 6"......................................$150.00 – 175.00
2. Pitcher, 7"......................................$350.00 – 400.00

3. Pitcher, 6".....................................$100.00 – 125.00

Row 2:
1. Pitcher, 7½".....................................$150.00 – 175.00
2. Pitcher, 7½", R #18 ....$100.00 – 125.00
3. Pitcher, 7½".....................................$150.00 – 175.00

Row 3:
1. Pitcher, 7½".....................................$300.00 – 350.00
2. Pitcher, 6½" (rare) ....$350.00 – 400.00
3. Pitcher, 7½".....................................$400.00 – 450.00

Page 53, Blended Glaze & Early Pitchers
Row 1:
1. Vase, 7"..$75.00 – 100.00
2. Tankard, 12", #890 ....$150.00 – 200.00
3. Vase, 6½"...$75.00 – 100.00

Row 2:
1. Pitcher, 3"......................................$60.00 – 70.00
2. Vase, 3"..$75.00 – 85.00
3. Vase, 5½"...$85.00 – 95.00
4. Vase, 4", #817 ....$95.00 – 110.00

Row 3:
1. Pitcher, 6½".....................................$400.00 – 450.00
2. Pitcher, 7"......................................$100.00 – 125.00
3. Pitcher, 6"......................................$100.00 – 125.00

Row 4:
1. Pitcher, 7½".....................................$125.00 – 150.00
2. Pitcher, with gold tracing, 9"..................$150.00 – 175.00
3. Pitcher, 9½".....................................$150.00 – 200.00
4. Rozane Pitcher, 8½", #886 ....$400.00 – 500.00

Page 54, Canvassers Outfit, before 1898
Row 1:
1. Apple Bank, 2¾" x 3½" ....$350.00 – 400.00

Row 2:
1. Apple Bank, 3" x 4" ....$350.00 – 400.00
2. Orange Bank, 3¼" x 3½" ....$350.00 – 400.00

Page 55, Banks
Row 1:
1. Jug, 4"...$100.00 – 125.00
2. Monkey bottle, 5½"...............................$100.00 – 125.00
3. Monkey, 6", rare glaze ....$450.00 – 500.00
4. Monkey bottle, 5½"...............................$100.00 – 125.00

Row 2:
1. Eagle, 2½".......................................$350.00 – 400.00
2. Lion, 2½"...$350.00 – 400.00
3. Cat, 4"..$550.00 – 600.00
4. Beehive, 3".....................................$400.00 – 450.00
5. Beehive, 2½".....................................$350.00 – 400.00

Row 1:
1. Pig, 2½" x 5"...................................$150.00 – 200.00
2. Large Pig, 4" x 5½".............................$350.00 – 400.00
3. Pig, 3" x 4"....................................$175.00 – 200.00

Row 2:
1. Buffalo, 3" x 6" ....$350.00 – 400.00
2. Dog, 4" ....$550.00 – 600.00
3. Uncle Sam, 4" ....$150.00 – 175.00
4. Buffalo, 3" x 6½" ....$350.00 – 400.00

Page 56, Cremo
Vase, 7" ....$2,500.00 – 3,000.00

Autumn
Row 1:
1. Pitcher, 8½" ....$400.00 – 450.00
2. Toothbrush holder, 5" ....$275.00 – 325.00
3. Shaving mug, 4" ....$275.00 – 325.00
4. Soap dish/liner, 5½" across ....$300.00 – 350.00

Row 2:
1. Wash bowl, 14½" ....$300.00 – 350.00
2. Pitcher, 12½" ....$450.00 – 500.00
   Set ....$850.00 – 1,000.00
3. Jardiniere, 9½" ....$600.00 – 700.00

Page 57, Sylvan
1. Vase, 9½" ....$500.00 – 600.00
2. Jardiniere, 9" ....$500.00 – 600.00

Tourist Variation
Unusual vase, 9" ....$500.00 – 600.00

Tourist
1. Window box, 8½" x 19" ....$5,000.00 – 6,000.00
2. Vase, 8" ....$1,500.00 – 2,000.00

Page 58, Novelty Steins
Choice..$250.00 – 300.00

Page 59, Smoker Sets
Row 1:
1. Ashtray, 2" ....$75.00 – 85.00
2. Ashtray, 3" ....$200.00 – 250.00
3. Indian smoker set, 4½" x 6½" ....$350.00 – 400.00
4. Ashtray, 2" ....$60.00 – 70.00

Row 2:
Ashtrays, 2", each................................$60.00 – 70.00
1. Tobacco jar, 6" ....$250.00 – 300.00
2. Combination set, 7½" ....$400.00 – 500.00
3. Combination set, 7½" ....$275.00 – 350.00
4. Jar, 4½" ....$125.00 – 150.00

Page 60, Donatella Tea Sets
Row 1:
Set ....$300.00 – 350.00
Creamer, 3"..$60.00 – 70.00
Sugar with lid, 3½" ....$70.00 – 80.00

Row 2:
Set ....$275.00 – 300.00

Creamer, 3" ....$60.00 – 70.00
Sugar with lid, 3" ....$70.00 – 80.00

Row 3:
Set ....$300.00 – 325.00
Creamer, 2½" ....$60.00 – 70.00
Sugar with lid, 3½" ....$70.00 – 80.00

Row 4:
Set ....$250.00 – 275.00
Creamer, 3" ....$45.00 – 55.00
Sugar with lid, 4" ....$55.00 – 65.00

Row 5:
Set ....$400.00 – 450.00
Creamer, 3" ....$75.00 – 90.00
Sugar with lid, 4" ....$100.00 – 110.00

Page 61, Creamware
Row 1:
Persian Tea set; Creamer, 3" ....$75.00 – 100.00
Persian Tea set; Teapot, 4½" ....$175.00 – 200.00
Persian Tea set; Chocolate pot, 6½" ....$200.00 – 250.00
Persian Tea set; Sugar, 4" ....$75.00 – 100.00

Row 2:
1. Stylized Crocus motif; Creamer, 3".............$60.00 – 75.00
2. Stylized Crocus motif; Sugar, 4½" ....$60.00 – 75.00
3. Good Night candlestick, 7"....................$450.00 – 500.00
4. Pitcher, 5"..$100.00 – 150.00

Row 3:
1. Pot/liner, 3½" ....$125.00 – 150.00
2. Pot/liner, 4" ....$175.00 – 225.00
3. Pot/liner, 4" ....$75.00 – 100.00
4. Pot/liner, 3½" ....$125.00 – 150.00

Row 4:
1. Cherries motif Teapot, 8½" ....$500.00 – 600.00
2. Trivet, 6" ....$250.00 – 300.00
3. Pitcher, 8"..$200.00 – 250.00

Page 62, Gold Traced and Decorated and Gold Traced
1. Candlestick, 9"......................................$100.00 – 125.00
2. Candlestick, 9"......................................$125.00 – 150.00
3. Candlestick, 4"......................................$125.00 – 150.00
4. Candlestick, 9"......................................$150.00 – 175.00
5. Candlestick, 8½"....................................$150.00 – 175.00

Dutch
Row 1:
1. Shaving mug, 4" ....$100.00 – 125.00
2. Pitcher, 7½"...$175.00 – 225.00
3. Child's teapot, 4½" ....$250.00 – 275.00

Row 2:
1. Pin tray, 4" ....$65.00 – 75.00
2. Teapot, 6½"...$350.00 – 400.00
3. Toothbrush holder, 4".............................$75.00 – 100.00

Page 63, Dutch
Row 1:

Child's creamer, 1½" ....$100.00 – 125.00
Teapot, 4" ....$200.00 – 250.00
Sugar, 3" ....$100.00 – 125.00

Row 2:

1. Child's soap dish with lid, 3" ....$250.00 – 275.00
   Child's milk pitcher, 4½" ....$250.00 – 275.00
   Child's tumbler, 4" ....$225.00 – 250.00
   Child's tumbler, 4" ....$200.00 – 225.00

Row 3:

1. Humidor, 6" ....$200.00 – 250.00
2. Plate, 11" ....$100.00 – 125.00
3. Child's creamer, 3" ....$200.00 – 225.00
4. Teapot, 7" ....$400.00 – 450.00

Row 4:

1. Child's combinet, 10½" ....$350.00 – 400.00
2. Child's potty, 5½" ....$300.00 – 350.00
3. Tankard, 11½" ....$150.00 – 175.00

Page 64, Creamware
Row 1:

1. Mug, 5" ....$100.00 – 125.00
2. Mug, 5" ....$225.00 – 275.00
3. Mug, 5" ....$250.00 – 275.00
4. Mug, 5" ....$100.00 – 125.00

Row 2:

1. Custard cup, 2½" ....$50.00 – 60.00
2. Tumbler, 4" ....$100.00 – 125.00
3. Jardiniere/liner, 4" ....$100.00 – 125.00
4. Jardiniere/liner, 3½" ....$100.00 – 125.00
5. Mug, 3½" ....$400.00 – 450.00

Row 3:

1. Pitcher, 6" ....$275.00 – 325.00
2. Coffeepot, 10" ....$800.00 – 900.00
3. Ceramic Design teapot, 9" ....$400.00 – 450.00

Row 4:

1. Indian decal mug, 5" ....$150.00 – 175.00
2. Tankard, 11½" ....$300.00 – 350.00
3. Mug, 5" ....$150.00 – 175.00
4. Mug, 5" ....$150.00 – 175.00
5. Tankard, 11½" ....$200.00 – 250.00
6. Mug, 5" ....$100.00 – 125.00

Page 65, Stein sets
Row 1:

1. Mug, 5" ....$100.00 – 125.00
2. Mug, 5" ....$225.00 – 275.00
3. Mug, 5" ....$125.00 – 150.00

Row 2:

Mugs, 5", each ....$175.00 – 200.00

Row 3:

1. Mug, 5", ...$150.00 – 175.00

2. Mug, 5" ....$200.00 – 250.00
3. Tankard, 12" ....$300.00 – 350.00
4. Tankard, 12" ....$175.00 – 200.00
5. Mug, 5" ....$100.00 – 125.00
6. Mug, 5" ....$150.00 – 175.00

Row 4:

1. Tankard, 12" ....$200.00 – 250.00
2. Tankard, 12" ....$400.00 – 450.00
3. Tankard, 11½" ....$225.00 – 275.00
4. Tankard, 10½" ....$300.00 – 350.00
5. Tankard, 10½" ....$250.00 – 300.00

Page 66, Creamware
Row 1:

1. Holly Tumbler, 4" ....$200.00 – 250.00
2. Medallion Pitcher, 3½" ....$100.00 – 125.00
3. Medallion Creamer, 3" medallion ....$75.00 – 85.00
4. Creamer, 3½" ....$75.00 – 85.00
5. Quaker Children hair receiver, 2" ....$100.00 – 125.00

Row 2:

1. Toothbrush holder, 5" ....$150.00 – 175.00
2. Mug, 5" ....$100.00 – 125.00
3. Mug, 5" ....$100.00 – 125.00
4. Mug, 5" ....$100.00 – 125.00

Dog dishes
Row 3:

1. 3" x 8½" ....$500.00 – 600.00
2. 2" x 5½" ....$400.00 – 500.00

Watch fob
¾" across ....$400.00 – 500.00

Page 67, Creamware
Row 1:

1. Ring tree, 3½" ....$100.00 – 125.00
2. Pin box, 4" ....$175.00 – 225.00
3. Cake plate, 10" ....$200.00 – 250.00
4. Candlesticks, 2", each ....$125.00 – 150.00

Row 2:

1. Pitcher, 7" ....$200.00 – 250.00
2. Cuspidor, 10" ....$400.00 – 450.00
3. Flower arranger, 2-piece, 2" ....$100.00 – 125.00
4. Flower arranger, 2-piece, 2" ....$100.00 – 125.00

Row 3:

1. Tankard, 12" ....$225.00 – 275.00
2. Mug, 5" ....$150.00 – 175.00
3. Tankard, 11½" ....$300.00 – 350.00
4. Mug, 5" ....$150.00 – 175.00
5. Tankard, 11½" ....$300.00 – 350.00

Page 68
Old Ivory, Ivory Tint

1. Compote, 9" ....$150.00 – 200.00
2. Pot, 3½" ....$95.00 – 110.00

Creamware
1. Persian-type pot, 8"................................$175.00 – 225.00
2. Plate with nude, 8"..............................$450.00 – 550.00
3. Coffeepot, 10"....................................$400.00 – 450.00

Holly
1. Chamberstick, 7" ....$500.00 – 600.00
2. Teapot, 4½"..$300.00 – 350.00
3. Creamer, 3" ....$175.00 – 200.00
4. Reverse side of chamberstick ....$500.00 – 600.00

Page 69, Old Ivory, Ivory Tint
Row 1:
1. Planter, 4"..$75.00 – 85.00
2. Humidor, 6" ....$225.00 – 275.00
3. Double bud vase, 5" x 6½"....................$100.00 – 125.00

Row 2:
1. Jardiniere/liner, 8", #513 ....$250.00 – 300.00
2. Tankard, 13½".....................................$300.00 – 350.00
3. Jardiniere, 9" ....$275.00 – 325.00

Forget-Me-Not
1. Sugar, 3" ....$100.00 – 125.00
2. Creamer, 1½".....................................$100.00 – 125.00

Page 70, Persian
1. Jardiniere, 5" ....$350.00 – 400.00
2. Hanging basket, 9" ....$400.00 – 500.00
3. Jardiniere, 8" ....$450.00 – 500.00

1. Jardiniere, 6½", #462-7 ....$350.00 – 400.00
2. Candlestick, 8½"..................................$125.00 – 150.00
3. Jardiniere, 5" ....$250.00 – 300.00

Page 71, Blended Glaze
1. Jardiniere, base diameter 4¼"..................$75.00 – 100.00
2. Jardiniere and pedestal, 12"...................$250.00 – 300.00
3. Jardiniere, 5½"....................................$100.00 – 125.00

Ceramic Design
1. Tumblers, 4", each ....$100.00 – 125.00
2. Pitcher, 6½".......................................$250.00 – 300.00

Page 72
Row 1:
1. Cuspidor, 5" ....$100.00 – 125.00
2. Gold Traced Cuspidor, 5" ....$175.00 – 200.00
3. Fern Trail Cuspidor, 5" ....$125.00 – 150.00

Row 2:
1. Mercian Jardiniere, 8" ....$1,000.00 – 1,250.00
2. Old Ivory Jardiniere, 8" ....$200.00 – 250.00

Row 3:
1. Decorated Matt Jardiniere, 9"..........$1,000.00 – 1,250.00
2. Decorated Matt Jardiniere, 8"..........$1,000.00 – 1,250.00

Venetian
1. Bake pan, 7" ....$50.00 – 60.00
2. Pudding crock....................................$40.00 – 50.00
3. Bake pan, 9" ....$55.00 – 65.00

Page 73, Pitchers
Row 1:
Pitcher, 6½".....................................$125.00 – 150.00
Bowl, 5½" x 9½"...............................$80.00 – 100.00
Pitcher, 6½".....................................$125.00 – 150.00

Row 2:
1. Pitcher, 7½".......................................$125.00 – 150.00
2. Pitcher, 7½".......................................$100.00 – 125.00
3. Pitcher, 6"..$100.00 – 125.00

Row 1:
1. Bake Pan, 3" x 10" ....$75.00 – 85.00
2. Pitcher, 8"..$125.00 – 150.00

Row 2:
1. Mug, 3½"...$60.00 – 70.00
2. Mug, 4"...$60.00 –70.00
3. Mug, 5" ....$60.00 – 70.00
4. Mug, 6" ....$75.00 – 85.00
5. Pitcher, 7½".......................................$100.00 – 125.00

Page 74, Juvenile
Row 1:
1. Fat Puppy Mug, 3½"............................$600.00 – 700.00
2. Fat Puppy Pitcher, 3½".........................$600.00 – 700.00
3. Fat Puppy Plate, 7".............................$600.00 – 700.00
4. Sad Puppy Creamer, 3½"......................$500.00 – 600.00
5. Sad Puppy Bowl, 4½"...........................$600.00 – 700.00

Row 2:
1. Duck with Boots Creamer, 3" ....$250.00 – 300.00
2. Duck with Boots Bowl, 5".....................$250.00 – 300.00
3. Chicks Rolled-edge Plate, 8".................$250.00 – 300.00
4. Chicks Bowl, 6" ....$250.00 – 300.00
5. Chicks Creamer, 3" ....$200.00 – 250.00

Row 3:
1. Chicks Custard, 2½" ....$300.00 – 350.00
2. Chicks Creamer, 3" ....$150.00 – 200.00
3. Chicks Small Rolled-edge Plate, 7"........$150.00 – 200.00
4. Chicks Pitcher, 3"...............................$150.00 – 200.00
5. Chicks Bowl, 4½' ....$150.00 – 200.00
6. Chicks Cup, 2"; Saucer, 5½" ....$250.00 – 300.00

Row 4:
1. Chicks Baby's Plate, 8" ....$125.00 – 150.00
2. Chicks Egg Cup, 3½" ....$250.00 – 275.00
3. Chicks Cake Plate, 9½" ....$600.00 – 700.00
4. Chicks Pudding Dish, 3½"......................$250.00 – 275.00
5. Chicks Plate, 7" ....$150.00 – 200.00

Page 75, Juvenile
Row 1:
1. Bear Creamer, 4"................................$900.00 – 1,000.00

2. Bear Bowl, 6" ....$900.00 – 1,000.00
3. Bear Mug, 3½" ....$900.00 – 1,000.00

Row 2:
   1. Goose Cup, 2"; Saucer, 5½" ....$400.00 – 500.00
   2. Goose Teapot, 4" .... $800.00 – 900.00
   3. Goose Sugar, 3" ....$450.00 – 500.00

Row 3:
   1. Goose Mug, 3½" ....$450.00 – 500.00
   2. Goose Plate, 7" ....$450.00 – 500.00
   3. Goose Creamer, 4" ....$450.00 – 500.00
   4. Goose Custard, 2½" ....$550.00 – 600.00

Row 4:
   1. Rabbit Custard, 2½" ....$300.00 – 350.00
   2. Rabbit B & M set, Pitcher, 3" ....$150.00 – 175.00
   3. Rabbit B & M set, Bowl, 4½" ....$125.00 – 150.00
   4. Rabbit Creamer, 3½" ....$150.00 – 175.00
   5. Cup, 2", Saucer, 5" ....$200.00 – 250.00
   6. Pudding dish, 1½" x 3½" ....$150.00 – 275.00

Row 5:
   1. Egg cup, 3", rare..................................$800.00 – 1,000.00
   2. Rabbit Baby's plate, 7" ....$150.00 – 175.00
   3. Rabbit Baby's plate, 8" ....$150.00 – 175.00
   4. Rabbit Plate, 7" ....$150.00 – 175.00
   5. Rabbit Egg cup, 3½" ....$250.00 – 275.00

Page 76, Juvenile
   1. Rabbit Pitcher, 7½" ....$1,500.00 – 1,750.00
   2. Rabbit Bowl, 10½" ....$1,000.00 – 1,250.00

Row 1:
   1. Chick Creamer, 3" ....$300.00 – 350.00
   2. Chick Teapot, 5", #8 ....$700.00 – 800.00
   3. Chick Sugar, 4" ....$400.00 – 450.00

Baby Bunting
Rows 2 & 3:
   1. Rolled-edge plates, 8", each ....$250.00 – 300.00

Page 77, Juvenile
Row 1, Skinny Puppy
   1. 2-handled Mug, 3" ....$150.00 – 175.00
   2. Rolled-edge plate, 8" ....$125.00 – 150.00
   3. Cup, 2"; Saucer, 5" ....$175.00 – 200.00
   4. Plate, 8"...$125.00 – 150.00
   5. Creamer, 3½" ....$125.00 – 150.00

Row 2, Early Duck with Hat
   1. Creamer, 3½" ....$100.00 – 125.00
   2. Cup, 2"; Saucer, 3" ....$150.00 – 175.00
   3. Rolled-edge plate, 8" ....$125.00 – 150.00
   4. Plate, 8"...$125.00 – 150.00
   5. 2-handled Mug, 3" ....$100.00 – 125.00
   6. Mug, 3" ....$100.00 – 125.00

Row 3, Sunbonnet Girl
   1. Creamer, 3½" ....$125.00 – 150.00
   2. Cup, 2"; Saucer, 3" ....$200.00 – 250.00

3. Rolled-edge plate, 8" ....$175.00 – 200.00
4. Plate, 8"...$175.00 – 200.00
5. Egg cup, 4", rare..................................$1,000.00 – 1,250.00
6. 2-handled Mug, 3' ....$250.00 – 300.00

Row 4:
   1. Experimental mug, 3"; Vitro #1237 ....$300.00 – 400.00
   2. Boxed set..$1,250.00 – 1,500.00
   3. Rabbit Potty, 3" x 6" ....$350.00 – 400.00
(add $300.00 for lid)

Page 78, Juvenile
Row 1:
   1. Nursery Rhyme motif; Set 3" sugar bowl, 6" teapot, and 3" creamer, rare, 3 pieces ....$1,000.00 – 1,250.00

Row 2:
   1. Santa Claus Creamer, 3½" ....$1,000.00 – 1,250.00
   2. Santa Claus Rolled-edge plate, 8" ...$1,250.00 – 1,500.00
   3. Santa Claus Cup, 2"; Saucer, 5".......$1,000.00 – 1,250.00

Row 3:
   1. Rabbit Mug, 3" ....$175.00 – 200.00
   2. Rabbit Rolled-edge plate, 8" ....$200.00 – 250.00
   3. Rabbit Egg Cup, 4" ....$1,000.00 – 1,250.00

Row 4:
   1. Pig Plate, 8" ....$1,250.00 – 1,500.00
   2. Pig Creamer, 4" ....$1,000.00 – 1,250.00
   3. Rooster Plate, 8" ....$1,500.00 – 2,000.00

Row 5:
   1. Fancy Cat Divided plate, 8½" ....$1,000.00 – 1,250.00
   2. Fancy Cat Rolled-edge plate, 8" ......$1,250.00 – 1,500.00
   3. Fancy Cat Plate, 8" ....$1,250.00 – 1,500.00
   4. Fancy Cat Mug, 3" ....$1,000.00 – 1,250.00

Page 79, Carnelian I
Row 1:
   1. Bowl/frog, 3" x 8½" ....$90.00 – 100.00
   2. Vase, 8" ....$100.00 – 125.00
   3. Fan vase, 6" ....$70.00 – 80.00
   4. Bowl, 3" x 9" ....$80.00 – 90.00

Row 2:
   1. Candle holder/frog, 3½" ....$70.00 – 80.00
   2. Pillow vase, 5".....................................$90.00 – 100.00
   3. Console, 5" x 12½" ....$125.00 – 150.00
   4. Flower frog, 4½" ....$75.00 – 85.00

Row 3:
   1. Vase, 7" ....$125.00 – 150.00
   2. Vase, 8" ....$125.00 – 150.00
   3. Vase, 7" ....$100.00 – 125.00
   4. Vase, 8" ....$150.00 – 200.00

Row 4:
   1. Vase, 9½" ....$200.00 – 250.00
   2. Vase, 10" ....$200.00 – 250.00
   3. Vase, 10" ....$200.00 – 250.00

Page 80, Carnelian II
Row 1:
    1. Vase, 5" ....$200.00 – 250.00
    2. Vase, 7" ....$200.00 – 250.00
    3. Planter, 3" x 8" ....$100.00 – 125.00

Row 2:
    1. Vase, 8" ....$350.00 – 400.00
    2. Vase, 6" ....$350.00 – 400.00
    3. Vase, 8" ....$350.00 – 400.00

Row 3:
    1. Vase, 7" ....$175.00 – 200.00
    2. Ewer, 12½" ....$600.00 – 700.00
    3. Vase, 10" ....$200.00 – 250.00
    4. Vase, 8" ....$200.00 – 250.00

Page 81, Carnelian II
Row 1:
    1. Vase, 12" ....$1,500.00 – 1,750.00
    2. Vase, 15" ....$1,750.00 – 2,000.00
    3. Vase, 12" ....$1,750.00 – 2,000.00

Row 2:
    1. Vase, 12" ....$1,500.00 –1,750.00
    2. Lamp base, 8" ....$900.00 – 1,000.00
    3. Vase, 14" ....$900.00 – 1,000.00

    1. Vase, 18½" ....$4,000.00 – 5,000.00
    2. Vase, 14½" ....$3,500.00 – 4,000.00

Page 82, Carnelian II
Row 1:
    1. Vase, 8" ....$175.00 – 225.00
    2. Basket, 4" x 10" ....$200.00 – 250.00
    3. Vase, 7" ....$150.00 – 175.00

Row 2:
    1. Bowl, 3" x 8" ....$100.00 – 125.00
    2. Bowl, 5" x 12½" ....$250.00 – 275.00
    3. Fan Vase, 6½" ....$100.00 – 125.00

Row 3:
    1. Bowl, 4" x 10" ....$200.00 – 250.00
    2. Bowl, 4" x 15" ....$300.00 – 350.00

Row 4:
    1. Vase, 9" ....$200.00 – 250.00
    2. Vase, 9" ....$200.00 – 250.00
    3. Vase, 8" ....$300.00 – 350.00
    4. Frog, 4" x 6" ....$100.00 – 150.00

Page 83, Mostique
    1. Jardiniere, 10" ....$1,500.00 – 1,750.00
    2. Metal stand, 38" ....$200.00 – 250.00

Page 84, Mostique
Row 1:
    1. Hanging basket, 7" ....$400.00 – 500.00

    2. Bowl, 7" ....$150.00 – 175.00
    3. Bowl, 7" ....$150.00 – 175.00
    4. Bowl, 5½" ....$125.00 – 150.00

Row 2:
    1. Bowl, 9½" ....$200.00 – 250.00
    2. Compote, 7" ....$300.00 – 350.00
    3. Bowl, 9" ....$350.00 – 400.00

Row 3:
    1. Vase, 10" ....$500.00 – 600.00
    2. Vase, 12" ....$900.00 – 1,000.00
    3. Jardiniere, 8" ....$250.00 – 300.00
    4. Vase, 6" ....$175.00 – 225.00

Page 85, Rosecraft Panel
Row 1:
    1. Vase, 6", brown ....$150.00 – 175.00
       green ....$200.00 – 250.00
    2. Covered jar, 10", brown ....$500.00 – 550.00
       green ....$600.00 – 700.00
    3. Bowl vase, 4", brown ....$150.00 – 175.00
       green ....$200.00 – 250.00

Row 2:
    1. Nude lamp base, 10", brown ....$1,250.00 – 1,500.00
       green ....$2,000.00 – 2,500.00
       red ....$2,500.00 – 3,000.00
    2. Window box, 6" x 12", brown ....$400.00 – 450.00
       green ....$500.00 – 550.00
    3. Vase, 10", brown ....$350.00 – 400.00
       green ....$450.00 – 500.00

Page 86, Imperial I
Row 1:
    1. Basket, 9", #7 ....$200.00 – 250.00
    2. Basket, 10", #8 ....$250.00 – 275.00
    3. Basket, 10", #9 ....$250.00 – 275.00
    4. Vase, 8" ....$175.00 – 225.00

Row 2:
    1. Vase, 10" ....$250.00 – 300.00
    2. Compote, 6½" ....$175.00 – 225.00
    3. Vase, 8" ....$225.00 – 275.00

Row 3:
    1. Vase, 10" ....$250.00 – 300.00
    2. Planter, 14" x 16" ....$350.00 – 400.00
    3. Vase, 12" ....$350.00 – 400.00

Page 87, Velmoss Scroll
Row 1:
    1. Vase, 5" ....$150.00 – 175.00
    2. Vase, 8" ....$200.00 – 250.00
    3. Bowl, 3", C7 ....$125.00 – 150.00

Row 2:
    1. Vase, 8" ....$200.00 – 250.00
    2. Vase, 10" ....$200.00 – 250.00
    3. Vase, 12" ....$400.00 – 450.00
    4. Vase, 10" ....$275.00 – 325.00

Page 88, Cameo II
Row 1:
Jardiniere, 8"h ....$450.00 – 550.00

Row 2:
Jardiniere, 9"h ....$550.00 – 650.00
Jardiniere, 9"h ....$650.00 – 750.00

Page 89, Cameo II
Row 1:
Flowerpot ....$350.00 – 450.00
Double bud vase ....$350.00 – 450.00

Row 2:
Vase, 7½" ....$500.00 – 600.00
Vase, 7½" ....$450.00 – 550.00

Row 3:
Wall pocket, 9½" ....$500.00 – 600.00
Hanging basket, 4½" x 7" ....$350.00 – 450.00

Page 90, Donatello
Row 1:
1. Powder jar, 2" x 5" ....$450.00 – 550.00
2. Vase, 6" ....$400.00 – 450.00
3. Double bud vase, 7" ....$400.00 – 450.00
4. Incense burner, 3½" ....$500.00 – 600.00

Row 2:
1. Vase, 8½" ....$350.00 – 400.00
2. Vase, 12" ....$350.00 – 400.00
3. Vase, 9½" ....$275.00 – 325.00
4. Plate, 8" ....$450.00 – 500.00

Stencil, 16½" x 3" ....$300.00 – 400.00
Light sconce, 18" x 6" ....$3,000.00 – 4,000.00

Page 91, Donatello
Row 1:
1. Bowl, 6" ....$75.00 – 95.00
2. Ashtray, 3" ....$175.00 – 225.00
3. Hanging basket, 7" ....$250.00 – 300.00
4. Ashtray, 3" ....$175.00 – 225.00
5. Ashtray, 2" ....$250.00 – 300.00

Row 2:
1. Rolled-edge bowl, 9½" ....$125.00 – 150.00
2. Bowl, 8½" x 3½", #238/7 ....$125.00 – 150.00
3. Bowl, 8" x 3" ....$125.00 – 150.00

Row 3:
1. Cuspidor, 5½" ....$300.00 – 350.00
2. Jardiniere, 6" ....$150.00 – 175.00
3. Compote, 5" ....$125.00 – 175.00
4. Candlestick, 6½" ....$175.00 – 225.00

Row 4:
1. Vase, 8" ....$95.00 – 110.00
2. Vase, 10" ....$150.00 – 175.00
3. Vase, 12" ....$200.00 – 250.00
4. Compote, 9½" ....$200.00 – 250.00
5. Basket, 7½" ....$350.00 – 400.00

Page 92, Rozane (1917)
Row 1:
1. Bowl, 3" ....$100.00 – 125.00
2. Compote, 8" ....$150.00 – 175.00
3. Vase, 6½" ....$100.00 – 125.00

Row 2:
1. Urn, 6½" ....$175.00 – 200.00
2. Footed bowl, 5" ....$175.00 – 200.00
3. Bowl, 3½" ....$100.00 – 125.00

Row 3:
1. Bowl, 5" ....$125.00 – 150.00
2. Compote, 6½" ....$150.00 – 175.00
3. Bowl, 4½" ....$125.00 – 150.00

Row 4:
1. Basket, 11" ....$300.00 – 350.00
2. Vase, 8" ....$150.00 – 175.00
3. Vase, 10" ....$200.00 – 250.00
4. Vase, 10" ....$200.00 – 250.00
5. Vase, 8" ....$150.00 – 175.00

Page 93, Azurine, Orchid, and Turquoise
1. Bud vases, 10", pair ....$100.00 – 150.00
2. Console bowl, 12½" ....$75.00 – 100.00

1. Double bud vase, 5" x 8" ....$125.00 – 150.00
2. Vase, 10" ....$150.00 – 175.00
3. Vase, 8" ....$75.00 – 100.00

Page 94, Rosecraft Blended
Row 1:
1. Vase, 6" ....$90.00 – 110.00
2. Window box, 5" x 8" ....$125.00 – 150.00
3. Jardiniere, 4" ....$90.00 – 110.00
4. Bud vase, #36-6 ....$90.00 – 110.00

Row 2:
1. Vase, 10", #35 ....$125.00 – 150.00
2. Vase, 8" ....$150.00 – 175.00
3. Vase, 12½" ....$150.00 – 175.00

Lombardy
1. Jardiniere, 6½" ....$200.00 – 250.00
2. Vase, 6" ....$200.00 – 250.00

Page 95, Rosecraft Black and Colors
Row 1:
1. Compote, 4" x 11" ....$125.00 – 150.00

Row 2:
1. Bowl, 3" x 8" ....$75.00 – 95.00
2. Double bud vase, 5" ....$125.00 – 150.00
3. Bowl/frog, 2" x 8½" ....$75.00 – 95.00

Row 3:
1. Bowl, 5" ....$125.00 – 150.00
2. Ginger jar, 8" ....$300.00 – 350.00
3. Bud vase, 8" ....$75.00 – 95.00
4. Flowerpot, 4½" ....$175.00 – 200.00

Row 4:
1. Vase, 10" ....$175.00 – 200.00
2. Vase, 13½" ....$250.00 – 300.00
3. Vase, 10" ....$175.00 – 200.00
4. Vase, 9" ....$175.00 – 200.00

Page 96, Rosecraft Vintage
Row 1:
1. Bowl, 3" ....$125.00 – 150.00
2. Vase, 6" ....$250.00 – 300.00
3. Vase, 4" ....$175.00 – 200.00

Row 2:
1. Vase, 8½" ....$400.00 – 450.00
2. Window box, 6" x 11½" ....$550.00 – 650.00
3. Vase, 12" ....$550.00 – 650.00

Page 97, Rosecraft Hexagon
Row 1:
1. Vase, 6", brown..................................$250.00 – 300.00
   green ....$350.00 – 400.00
   blue ....$450.00 – 500.00
2. Vase, 5", brown ....$200.00 – 250.00
   green ....$300.00 – 350.00
   blue ....$400.00 – 450.00
3. Vase, 5", blue hi-gloss glaze..................$400.00 – 500.00
4. Vase, 4", brown ....$175.00 – 225.00
   green ....$275.00 – 325.00
   blue ....$375.00 – 425.00
5. Bowl, 7½", brown ....$150.00 – 175.00
   green ....$250.00 – 275.00
   blue ....$350.00 – 375.00

Row 2:
1. Candlestick, 8", brown .... $350.00 – 400.00
   green ....$450.00 – 500.00
   blue ....$550.00 – 600.00
2. Vase, 8", brown..................................$350.00 – 400.00
   green ....$450.00 – 500.00
   blue ....$550.00 – 600.00
3. Double bud vase, 5", brown ....$350.00 – 400.00
   green ....$450.00 – 500.00
   blue ....$550.00 – 600.00
4. Vase, 8", brown..................................$350.00 – 400.00
   green ....$450.00 – 500.00
   blue ....$550.00 – 600.00
5. Candlestick, 8", brown.........................$350.00 – 400.00
   green ....$450.00 – 500.00
   blue ....$550.00 – 600.00

Page 98, Lustre
Row 1:
1. Basket, 10"..$200.00 – 250.00
2. Basket, 6"..$200.00 – 250.00

Row 2:
1. Bowl, 5"...$95.00 – 125.00
2. Vase, 12" ....$250.00 – 275.00
3. Candlestick, 10"...................................$100.00 – 125.00
4. Candlestick, 5½' ....$45.00 – 55.00

1. Vase, 12" ....$250.00 – 275.00
2. Basket, 6½"..$200.00 – 250.00

Page 99, Matt Color
1. Bowl, 3", #15 ....$70.00 – 80.00
2. Vase, 4" ....$70.00 – 80.00
3. Bowl, 4"...$70.00 – 80.00
4. Vase, 4" ....$70.00 – 80.00
5. Pot, 4" ....$70.00 – 80.00

Imperial II
1. Vase, 9" ....$1,250.00 – 1,500.00
2. Vase, 10", #477 ....$1,250.00 – 1,500.00
3. Vase, 8" ....$1,500.00 – 1,750.00
4. Vase, 8", #473 ....$1,500.00 – 1,750.00

Page 100, Imperial II
Row 1:
1. Bowl, 4½" ....$400.00 – 450.00
2. Vase, 5½" ....$250.00 – 300.00
3. Vase, 7" ....$400.00 – 450.00
4. Vase, 4½" ....$250.00 – 300.00
5. Vase, 6" ....$1,000.00 – 1,250.00

Row 2:
1. Bowl, 4½" ....$400.00 – 450.00
2. Vase, 5" ....$350.00 – 400.00
3. Bowl, 5" x 9" ....$1,500.00 – 1,750.00
4. Vase, 5" ....$1,500.00 – 1,750.00

Row 3:
1. Vase, 7" ....$500.00 – 550.00
2. Vase, 4" ....$500.00 – 550.00
3. Bowl, 5" x 12½", with frog.....................$500.00 – 550.00
4. Vase, 7" ....$350.00 – 400.00

Row 4:
1. Vase, 8½" ....$900.00 – 1,000.00
2. Vase, 8" ....$750.00 – 850.00
3. Vase, 11" ....$1,500.00 – 1,750.00
4. Vase, 8½" ....$1,200.00 – 1,400.00

Page 101, Dogwood I
Row 1:
1. Double bud vase, 8" ....$150.00 – 175.00
2. Tub, 4" x 7" ....$125.00 – 150.00

Row 2:
1. Window box/liner, 5½" x 13½" ....$350.00 – 400.00
2. Vase, 14½" ....$550.00 – 650.00

Dogwood II
Row 1:
1. Vase, 7" ....$200.00 – 250.00
2. Hanging basket, 7" ....$250.00 – 300.00
3. Bowl, 2½" ....$125.00 – 150.00

Row 2:
1. Bowl, 4" ....$125.00 – 150.00
2. Jardiniere, 6" ....$150.00 – 175.00
3. Jardiniere, 8" ....$250.00 – 300.00

Page 102, Dahlrose
Row 1:
1. Vase, 6", #418 .... $150.00 – 175.00
2. Hanging basket, 7½", #343 .... $250.00 – 300.00
3. Pillow vase, 5" x 7", #419 .... $200.00 – 250.00

Row 2:
1. Candlesticks, 3½", #1069, pair .... $175.00 – 225.00
2. Vase, 6", #364 .... $200.00 – 250.00
3. Bowl vase, 4", #420 .... $150.00 – 175.00

Row 3:
1. Vase, 8", #366 .... $225.00 – 275.00
2. Window box, 6" x 12½", #377 .... $350.00 – 400.00
3. Bud vase, 8", #78 .... $175.00 – 225.00

Row 4:
1. Window box, 6" x 16", #375-14 .... $350.00 – 400.00
2. Window box, 6" x 11½", #375-10 .... $300.00 – 350.00

Page 103, Cremona
1. Urn, 4" .... $150.00 – 175.00
2. Fan, 5" .... $125.00 – 150.00
3. Vase, 8" .... $200.00 – 250.00
4. Vase, 12" .... $350.00 – 400.00

Page 105, Florentine
1. Hanging basket, 9" diameter .... $275.00 – 325.00
2. Jardiniere, 5" .... $150.00 – 175.00
3. Ashtray, 5" .... $150.00 – 175.00
4. Vase, 8" .... $175.00 – 225.00

Row 2:
1. Bowl, 7" .... $100.00 – 125.00
2. Bowl, 9" .... $100.00 – 125.00
3. Bowl, 7" .... $100.00 – 125.00

Row 3:
1. Candlestick, 10½", each .... $150.00 – 175.00
2. Candlestick, 8½", each .... $125.00 – 150.00
3. Lamp base, 8" .... $400.00 – 500.00
4. Vase, 7" .... $175.00 – 225.00
5. Double bud vase, 4½" .... $100.00 – 125.00

Row 4:
1. Jardiniere, 5¾" base diameter .... $200.00 – 250.00
2. Window box, 11½" .... $300.00 – 350.00

Page 106, Vista
Row 1:
1. Basket, 12" .... $1,000.00 – 1,200.00
2. Vase, 10" .... $750.00 – 800.00
3. Basket, 9½" .... $900.00 – 1,000.00

Row 2:
1. Vase, 15", #121-5 .... $1,500.00 – 1,750.00
2. Vase, 18" .... $2,000.00 – 2,500.00
3. Vase, 18", #134-18 .... $1,750.00 – 2,000.00

Page 107, Victorian Art Pottery
Row 1:
1. Vase, 6" .... $500.00 – 550.00
2. Urn, 4" .... $350.00 – 400.00

Row 2:
1. Vase, 6" .... $400.00 – 450.00
2. Vase, 8" .... $550.00 – 600.00
3. Vase, 7" .... $500.00 – 550.00

Covered Jar, 8" .... $600.00 – 700.00

Page 108, Tuscany
Row 1:
1. Vase, 4", pink .... $100.00 – 125.00
   gray/lt. blue .... $75.00 – 100.00
2. Vase, 6", pink .... $125.00 – 150.00
   gray/lt. blue .... $100.00 – 125.00
3. Flower arranger, 5½", pink .... $100.00 – 125.00
   gray/lt. blue .... $75.00 – 100.00

Row 2:
1. Vase, 6", pink .... $125.00 – 150.00
   gray/lt. blue .... $100.00 – 125.00
2. Vase, 9", pink .... $200.00 – 225.00
   gray/lt. blue .... $150.00 – 175.00
3. Vase, 12", pink .... $300.00 – 350.00
   gray/lt. blue .... $225.00 – 250.00

Page 109, La Rose
Row 1:
1. Vase, 4" .... $125.00 – 150.00
2. Bowl, 3" .... $125.00 – 150.00

Row 2:
1. Wall pocket, 9" .... $300.00 – 350.00
2. Jardiniere, 6½" .... $150.00 – 175.00
3. Vase, 6" .... $150.00 – 175.00

Page 111, Volpato
Row 1:
Covered urn, 8" .... $300.00 – 350.00

Row 2:
1. Candlesticks, 9½", pair .... $250.00 – 275.00
2. Vase, 12" .... $250.00 – 300.00

Savona
Row 1:
1. Candlesticks, 3½", pair .... $125.00 – 150.00
2. Console bowl, 4" x 10" .... $125.00 – 150.00
3. Candlesticks, 3½", pair .... $200.00 – 250.00

Row 2:
1. Window box, 2½" x 9" .... $75.00 – 100.00
2. Flowerpot/saucer, 6" .... $250.00 – 300.00
3. Vase, 9" .... $150.00 – 175.00
4. Candlestick, 10", pair .... $200.00 – 250.00

Page 112, Corinthian
1. Vase, 8½" ....$150.00 – 175.00
2. Jardiniere, 7" ....$175.00 – 200.00

Row 1:
1. Wall pocket, 8" ....$275.00 – 325.00
2. Hanging basket, 8" ....$200.00 – 250.00
3. Wall pocket, 8½" ....$275.00 – 325.00

Row 2:
1. Footed bowl, 4½" ....$100.00 – 125.00
2. Vase, 6" ....$150.00 – 175.00
3. Vase, 7" ....$150.00 – 175.00
4. Bowl, 3" ....$75.00 – 95.00

Page 113, Normandy
Hanging basket, 7" $300.00

Florane
1. Bowl, 5" ....$125.00 – 150.00
2. Vase, 12½" ....$300.00 – 350.00
3. Basket, 8½" ....$300.00 – 350.00
4. Double bud vase, 5" ....$125.00 – 150.00

Page 114, Cherry Blossom
Hanging basket, 8", #350, brown ....$400.00 – 500.00
pink/blue ....$1,500.00 – 1,750.00

Page 115, Russco
Row 1:
1. Vase, 8", #61-183 ....$250.00 – 275.00
2. Vase, 7" ....$175.00 – 200.00

Row 2:
1. Double bud vase, 8½" ....$100.00 – 125.00
2. Vase, 9½" ....$150.00 – 175.00
3. Vase, 8½" ....$125.00 – 150.00

Row 3:
1. Vase, 7" ....$200.00 – 225.00
2. Vase, 12½" ....$450.00 – 500.00
3. Triple cornucopia, 8" x 12½" ....$300.00 – 350.00

Page 116, Wisteria
1. Vase, 10", #682, tan ....$750.00 – 850.00
blue ....$1,250.00 – 1,500.00
2. Hanging basket, 7½", #351, tan ....$1,000.00 – 1,250.00
blue ....$2,000.00 – 2,500.00

1. Vase, 8½", #635, tan ....$650.00 – 750.00
blue ....$900.00 – 1,000.00
2. Vase, 8½", #680, tan ....$700.00 – 800.00
blue ....$1,000.00 – 1,100.00
3. Bowl vase, 5", #632, tan ....$450.00 – 550.00
blue ....$700.00 – 800.00

Page 117, Jonquil
Row 1:
1. Bowl, 3", #523 ....$175.00 – 200.00

2. Candlestick, 4", #1082, pair ....$450.00 – 550.00
3. Center bowl, 3½" x 9", #219 ....$325.00 – 375.00
4. Vase, 4½", #101 ....$300.00 – 350.00
5. Vase, 4", #524 ....$250.00 – 275.00

Row 2:
1. Jardiniere, 4", #621 ....$250.00 – 275.00
2. Vase, 5½", #542 ....$375.00 – 450.00
3. Pot/frog, 5½", #94 ....$500.00 – 550.00
4. Vase, 4½", #93 ....$450.00 – 550.00

Row 3:
1. Vase, 7", #541 ....$400.00 – 475.00
2. Vase, 6½", #526 ....$450.00 – 550.00
3. Vase, 6½", #543 ....$450.00 – 550.00
4. Crocus pot, 7", #96 ....$1,000.00 – 1,100.00

Row 4:
1. Vase, 8", #528 ....$500.00 – 600.00
2. Vase, 9½", #544 ....$600.00 – 700.00
3. Vase, 12", #531 ....$1,250.00 – 1,500.00
4. Vase, 8", #529 ....$500.00 – 600.00

Page 118, Futura
1. Vase, 10", #434 ....$4,500.00 – 5,500.00
2. Vase, 12½", #394 ....$1,250.00 – 1,500.00

Page 119, Futura
Row 1:
1. Vase, 7½", #387 ....$1,100.00 – 1,200.00
2. Vase, 8", #386 ....$900.00 – 1,000.00
3. Vase, 7", #405 ....$900.00 – 1,000.00
4. Vase, 6", #380 ....$350.00 – 450.00
5. Pillow vase, 5" x 6", #81 ....$450.00 – 550.00

Row 2:
1. Vase, 4" x 6", #85 ....$400.00 – 500.00
2. Vase, 3½", #190 ....$400.00 – 500.00
3. Fan Vase, 6", #82 ....$550.00 – 650.00
4. Vase, 4", #189 ....$550.00 – 650.00

Row 3:
1. Window box, 5" x 15½", #376 ....$1,750.00 – 2,000.00
2. Candlestick, 4", #1072, pair ....$1,000.00 – 1,100.00
3. Jardiniere, 6", #616 ....$550.00 – 650.00

Row 4:
1. Vase, 6½", #421 ....$375.00 – 450.00
2. Vase, 5", #197 ....$800.00 – 900.00
3. Vase, 10", #392 ....$1,100.00 – 1,200.00
4. Vase, 8½", #406 ....$1,000.00 – 1,100.00
5. Vase, 7", #382 ....$375.00 – 450.00

Page 120, Futura
Row 1:
1. Vase, 5", #421 ....$375.00 – 450.00
2. Center bowl, 2½" x 10½", #195 ....$1,250.00 – 1,500.00
matching frog ....$400.00 – 500.00
3. Vase, 6", #423 ....$550.00 – 650.00

Row 2:
1. Bowl, 3½", #187 ....$550.00 – 650.00
    matching frog.............................$100.00 – 125.00
2. Bowl, 3½", #196 ....$700.00 – 800.00
    matching frog.............................$100.00 – 125.00
3. Bowl, 4", #188 ....$700.00 – 800.00
    matching frog...............................$75.00 – 100.00

Row 3:
1. Vase, 8", #384 ....$600.00 –700.00
2. Vase, 7½", #400 ....$1,000.00 – 1,100.00
3. Vase, 9½", #412 ....$12,500.00 – 15,000.00
4. Vase, 9", #409 ....$1,250.00 – 1,500.00

Row 4:
1. Vase, 9", #429 ....$1,500.00 – 1,750.00
2. Vase, 10", #432 ....$1,100.00 – 1,200.00
3. Vase, 15½", #438 ....$1,750.00 – 2,000.00
4. Vase, 10", #431 ....$900.00 – 1,000.00
5. Vase, 8", #402 ....$800.00 – 900.00

Page 121, Futura
1. Vase, 8", #383 ....$500.00 – 600.00
2. Vase, 7", #403 ....$1,100.00 – 1,200.00
3. Vase, 9", #388 ....$650.00 – 750.00

Row 2:
1. Vase, 9", #430 ....$1,750.00 – 2,000.00
2. Vase, 10", #435 ....$2,500.00 – 2,750.00
3. Vase, 8", #427 ....$1,250.00 – 1,500.00

Page 122, Laurel
1. Vase, 10", #676, gold ....$550.00 – 650.00
    russett ....$650.00 – 750.00
    green ....$800.00 – 900.00
2. Vase, 9½", #674, gold........................$500.00 – 600.00
    russett ....$600.00 – 700.00
    green ....$750.00 – 800.00
3. Vase, 6½", #250, gold........................$400.00 – 450.00
    russett ....$500.00 – 600.00
    green ....$650.00 – 750.00
4. Bowl, 3½", #252, gold ....$350.00 – 400.00
    russett ....$450.00 – 500.00
    green ....$500.00 – 550.00

Montacello
1. Basket, 6½", blue...........................$1,200.00 – 1,400.00
    tan ....$900.00 – 1,000.00
2. Vase, 5", blue ....$400.00 – 450.00
    tan ....$350.00 – 400.00
3. Vase, 8½", blue ....$650.00 – 750.00
    tan ....$550.00 – 600.00
4. Vase, 10½", blue ....$1,200.00 – 1,400.00
    tan ....$900.00 – 1,000.00

Page 123, Tourmaline
Row 1:
1. Vase, 5½" ....$100.00 – 125.00
2. Candlesticks, 5", pair........................$175.00 – 200.00
3. Pillow vase, 6"..............................$100.00 – 125.00
4. Vase, 6" ....$100.00 – 125.00

Row 2:
1. Vase, 4½"....................................$90.00 – 100.00
2. Vase, 7"....................................$125.00 – 150.00
3. Vase, 6"....................................$125.00 – 150.00
4. Bowl, 8"....................................$75.00 – 100.00

Row 3:
1. Cornucopia, 7" ....$75.00 – 100.00
2. Vase, 7" ....$75.00 – 100.00
3. Vase, 8" ....$150.00 – 175.00
4. Vase, 7½" ....$100.00 – 125.00
5. Vase, 5½" ....$80.00 – 100.00

Row 4:
1. Vase, 8" ....$100.00 – 125.00
2. Vase, 8" ....$150.00 – 175.00
3. Vase, 10" ....$250.00 – 275.00
4. Vase, 8" ....$150.00 – 175.00
5. Vase, 8" ....$150.00 – 175.00

Page 124, Velmoss
1. Vase, 14½", #722, green.........................$600.00 – 650.00
    blue ....$700.00 – 750.00
    red ....$800.00 – 850.00
    tan (rare) ....$900.00 – 950.00
2. Bowl, 3" x 11", #266, green...................$175.00 – 225.00
    blue ....$225.00 – 275.00
    red ....$275.00 – 325.00
    tan (rare) ....$325.00 – 375.00
1. Vase, 8", #718, green.........................$225.00 – 275.00
    blue ....$300.00 – 350.00
    red ....$350.00 – 400.00
    tan (rare) ....$400.00 – 450.00
2. Vase, 12½", #721, green......................$400.00 – 450.00
    blue ....$500.00 – 550.00
    red ....$550.00 – 600.00
    tan (rare) ....$600.00 – 650.00
3. Vase, 9½", #719, green.......................$275.00 – 325.00
    blue ....$350.00 – 400.00
    red ....$400.00 – 450.00
    tan (rare) ....$450.00 – 500.00

Page 125, Sunflower
Row 1:
1. Vase, 4" ....$600.00 – 700.00
2. Vase, 5" ....$600.00 – 700.00
3. Vase, 5" ....$600.00 – 700.00
4. Bowl, 4" ....$650.00 – 750.00

Row 2:
1. Candlesticks, 4", pair.......................$1,000.00 – 1,200.00
2. Center bowl, 3" x 12½" ....$900.00 – 1,000.00

Row 3:
1. Vase, 5", #486..............................$800.00 – 900.00
2. Window box, 3½" x 11" ....$900.00 – 1,000.00
3. Vase, 6" ....$600.00 – 700.00

Row 4:
1. Vase, 7", #489 ....$1,700.00 – 2,250.00
2. Vase, 10", #494 ....$2,000.00 – 2,500.00
3. Vase, 6", #619 ....$1,250.00 – 1,500.00

Page 126, Pine Cone
Row 1:
1. Planter, 5", #124, green ....$175.00 – 225.00
   brown ....$200.00 – 250.00
   blue ....$250.00 – 300.00
2. Centerpiece/candle holder, 6", #324,
   green ....$550.00 – 650.00
   brown ....$650.00 – 750.00
   blue ....$1,000.00 – 1,100.00
3. Bowl, 4½", #320-5, green ....$175.00 – 225.00
   brown ....$200.00 – 250.00
   blue ....$250.00 – 300.00

Row 2:
1. Bowl, 4½", #457-7, green ....$200.00 – 250.00
   brown ....$250.00 – 300.00
   blue ....$300.00 – 350.00
2. Window box, 3½" x 15½", #431-15,
   green ....$275.00 – 325.00
   brown ....$350.00 – 400.00
   blue ....$575.00 – 650.00
3. Ashtray, 4½", #499, green ....$150.00 – 175.00
   brown ....$175.00 – 200.00
   blue ....$200.00 – 225.00

Row 3:
1. Candlestick, 2½", #112-3, pair, green ....$125.00 – 150.00
   brown ....$150.00 – 175.00
   blue ....$175.00 – 200.00
2. Mug, 4", #960-4, green ....$300.00 – 350.00
   brown ....$350.00 – 400.00
   blue ....$400.00 – 450.00
3. Pitcher, 9½", #708-9, green ....$600.00 – 650.00
   brown ....$700.00 – 750.00
   blue ....$1,250.00 – 1,500.00
4. Tumbler, 5", #414, green ....$200.00 – 250.00
   brown ....$250.00 – 300.00
   blue ....$375.00 – 425.00
5. Candlestick, 5", #1099-4½, pair, green ..$175.00 – 200.00
   brown ....$225.00 – 275.00
   blue ....$275.00 – 350.00

Row 4:
1. Vase, 10½", #747-10, green ....$400.00 – 500.00
   brown ....$500.00 – 550.00
   blue ....$850.00 – 950.00
2. Vase, 14½", #850-14, green ....$650.00 – 750.00
   brown ....$800.00 – 900.00
   blue ....$1,500.00 – 1,750.00
3. Pitcher, 10½", #485-10, green ....$550.00 – 650.00
   brown ....$650.00 – 750.00
   blue ....$950.00 – 1,150.00

Page 127, Pine Cone
Row 1:
1. Bud vase, 7½", #479-7,
   Apple Blossom Pink.....................$1,500.00 – 2,000.00
2. Pillow vase, 8", #845-8, green.............$425.00 – 475.00
   brown ....$500.00 – 550.00
   blue ....$750.00 – 850.00
3. Boat dish, 9", #427-2, green.............$325.00 – 350.00
   brown ....$400.00 – 450.00
   blue ....$600.00 – 700.00

Row 2:
1. Vase, 7", #907-7, green ....$200.00 – 250.00
   brown ....$275.00 – 325.00
   blue ....$375.00 – 450.00
2. Center bowl, 11", green....................$225.00 – 275.00
   brown ....$275.00 – 325.00
   blue ....$400.00 – 450.00
3. Vase, 7", #121-7, green ....$225.00 – 275.00
   brown ....$275.00 – 325.00
   blue ....$400.00 – 450.00
4. Vase, 8½", #490-8, green ....$300.00 – 350.00
   brown ....$400.00 – 450.00
   blue ....$575.00 – 650.00

Row 3:
1. Vase, 7", #745-7, green ....$375.00 – 425.00
   brown ....$475.00 – 525.00
   blue ....$750.00 – 850.00
2. Double tray, 13", #462, green ....$375.00 – 425.00
   brown ....$475.00 – 525.00
   blue ....$750.00 – 850.00
3. Vase, 5", #261, green.......................$225.00 – 250.00
   brown ....$275.00 – 325.00
   blue ....$450.00 – 500.00

Row 4:
1. Vase, 8", #706, green............................$325.00 – 375.00
   brown ....$425.00 – 475.00
   blue ....$650.00 – 750.00
2. Basket, 11", #353-11, green.................$425.00 – 475.00
   brown ....$500.00 – 550.00
   blue ....$950.00 – 1,100.00
3. Vase, 8", #908-8, green ....$325.00 – 375.00
   brown ....$400.00 – 450.00
   blue ....$650.00 – 750.00

Page 128, Artcraft
   Jardiniere, 4", red............................$150.00 – 175.00
   tan ....$200.00 – 250.00
   blue/green ....$250.00 – 300.00

Page 129, Topeo
Row 1:
   Center bowl, 3" x 11½", red ....$100.00 – 125.00
   blue ....$200.00 – 250.00

Row 2:
1. Vase, 7", red.................................$150.00 – 200.00
   blue ....$350.00 – 400.00
2. Center bowl, 4" x 13", red ....$250.00 – 300.00
   blue ....$400.00 – 450.00
3. Vase, 6", red.................................$250.00 – 300.00
   blue ....$450.00 – 500.00

Row 3:
1. Vase, 14", red................................$900.00 – 1,000.00
   blue ....$2,000.00 – 2,500.00
2. Vase, 9", red.................................$275.00 – 325.00
   blue ....$500.00 – 550.00
3. Vase, 15", red...............................$1,500.00 – 2,000.00
   blue ....$3,500.00 – 4,000.00

1. Center bowl, 13", red............................$250.00 – 300.00
   blue...$400.00 – 450.00
2. Double candlestick, 5", pair, red............$300.00 – 350.00
   blue...$550.00 – 600.00

   Vase, 9", red..$325.00 – 375.00
   blue...$600.00 – 700.00
   trial color, yellow ....$1,250.00 – 1,500.00

Page 130, Moss
Row 1:
1. Bowl vase, 6", #290, pink/ or
   orange/green...$350.00 – 400.00
   blue...$300.00 – 350.00
2. Pillow vase, 8", #781-8, pink/ or
   orange/green...$350.00 – 400.00
   blue...$300.00 – 350.00
3. Candlesticks, 2", #1109, pair, pink/
   or orange/green ....$200.00 – 225.00
   blue...$150.00 – 175.00
4. Triple candlesticks, 7", #1108, pair, pink/
   or orange/green ....$800.00 – 900.00
   blue...$600.00 – 700.00

Luffa
Row1:
1. Vase, 8", #689 ....$650.00 – 750.00
2. Jardiniere, 7", #631 ....$350.00 – 400.00
3. Vase, 6", #683 ....$350.00 – 400.00
4. Candlesticks 5", #1097, pair...................$500.00 – 600.00

Row 2:
1. Lamp, 9½", blue/green glaze............$1,200.00 – 1,400.00
2. Vase, 15½".....................................$1,750.00 – 2,000.00
3. Lamp, 9½", blue/rose glaze..............$1,200.00 – 1,400.00

Page 131, Clemana
Row 1:
1. Bowl, 4½" x 6½", #281, blue.................$250.00 – 275.00
   green ....$225.00 – 250.00
   tan ....$200.00 – 225.00
2. Vase, 7½", #112, blue.........................$450.00 – 500.00
   green ....$350.00 – 400.00
   tan ....$300.00 – 350.00
3. Flower frog, 4", #23, blue ....$200.00 – 225.00
   green ....$175.00 – 200.00
   tan ....$150.00 – 175.00

Row 2:
1. Vase, 6½", #749, blue.........................$250.00 – 275.00
   green ....$225.00 – 250.00
   tan ....$200.00 – 225.00
2. Vase, 6½", #280, blue.........................$400.00 – 450.00
   green ....$350.00 – 400.00
   tan ....$300.00 – 350.00
3. Vase, 7½", #752, blue.........................$300.00 – 350.00
   green ....$250.00 – 300.00
   tan ....$225.00 – 250.00
4. Vase, 6½", #750, blue.........................$250.00 – 275.00
   green ....$225.00 – 250.00
   tan ....$200.00 – 225.00

Row 3:
1. Vase, 8½", #754, blue..........................$500.00 – 550.00
   green ....$450.00 – 500.00
   tan ....$400.00 – 450.00
2. Vase, 12½", #758, blue........................$600.00 – 650.00
   green ....$550.00 – 600.00
   tan ....$500.00 – 550.00
3. Vase, 14", #757, blue..........................$700.00 – 800.00
   green ....$600.00 – 700.00
   tan ....$500.00 – 600.00
4. Vase, 9½", #756, blue..........................$550.00 – 600.00
   green ....$500.00 – 600.00
   green ....$500.00 – 550.00
   tan ....$450.00 – 550.00

Page 132, Orian
Row 1:
1. Vase, 6", #733, tan..............................$150.00 – 175.00
   turquoise ....$175.00 – 200.00
   yellow ....$200.00 – 225.00
   red ....$225.00 – 250.00
2. Vase, 9", #738, tan..............................$275.00 – 325.00
   turquoise ....$325.00 – 350.00
   yellow ....$350.00 – 375.00
   red ....$375.00 – 400.00
3. Candle Holder, 4½", #1108, pair, tan......$250.00 – 300.00
   turquoise ....$275.00 – 325.00
   yellow ....$300.00 – 350.00
   red ....$325.00 – 375.00

Row 2:
1. Vase, 7", #734, tan..............................$175.00 – 200.00
   turquoise ....$200.00 – 225.00
   yellow ....$225.00 – 250.00
   red ....$250.00 – 275.00
2. Center Bowl, 5" x 12", #275, tan...........$250.00 – 275.00
   turquoise ....$275.00 – 300.00
   yellow ....$300.00 – 325.00
   red ....$325.00 – 350.00
3. Vase, 6½", #733, tan...........................$150.00 – 175.00
   turquoise ....$175.00 – 200.00
   yellow ....$200.00 – 225.00
   red ....$225.00 – 250.00

Page 133, Orian
1. Vase, 12½", #742, tan...........................$400.00 – 450.00
   turquoise ....$425.00 – 475.00
   yellow ....$475.00 – 525.00
   red ....$525.00 – 600.00
2. Vase, 10½", #740, tan..........................$275.00 – 325.00
   turquoise ....$325.00 – 350.00
   yellow ....$350.00 – 375.00
   red ....$375.00 – 400.00
3. Vase, 7½", #737, tan...........................$375.00 – 425.00
   turquoise ....$425.00 – 450.00
   yellow ....$450.00 – 475.00
   red ....$475.00 – 500.00
4. Compote, 4½" x 10½", #272, tan..........$175.00 – 200.00
   turquoise ....$200.00 – 225.00
   yellow ....$225.00 – 250.00
   red ....$250.00 – 275.00

Page 134, Falline
Row 1:
1. Vase, 6", #650, blue..........................$1,500.00 – 1,750.00
   tan..$600.00 – 700.00
2. Vase, 6", #642, blue..........................$1,000.00 – 1,100.00
   tan..$500.00 – 550.00
3. Candle holder, 4", #1092, pair, blue .$1,250.00 – 1,500.00
   tan..$800.00 – 1,000.00
4. Bowl, 11", #244, blue..........................$500.00 – 600.00
   tan..$350.00 – 450.00

Row 2:
1. Vase, 8", #646, blue..........................$1,200.00 – 1,400.00
   tan..$600.00 – 700.00
2. Vase, 12½", #653, blue....................$2,000.00 – 2,250.00
   tan..$1,000.00 – 1,100.00
3. Vase, 9", #652, blue..........................$1,750.00 – 2,000.00
   tan..$900.00 – 1,000.00
4. Vase, 7½", #647, blue....................$1,300.00 – 1,500.00
   tan..$600.00 – 700.00

Page 135, Ferella
Row 1:
1. Vase, 6", #505, tan............................$700.00 – 800.00
   red..$1,200.00 – 1,300.00
2. Lamp base, 10½", any color.............$1,000.00 – 1,250.00
3. Vase, 8", #508, tan............................$900.00 – 1,000.00
   red..$1,300.00 – 1,400.00

Row 2:
1. Vase, 6", #499, tan............................$400.00 – 500.00
   red..$550.00 – 650.00
2. Candlesticks, 4½", #1078, pair, tan.......$700.00 – 800.00
   red..$1,000.00 – 1,100.00
3. Bowl/frog, 5", #211, tan............$700.00 – 800.00
   red..$1,100.00 – 1,200.00
4. Vase, 4", #498, tan............................$350.00 – 400.00
   red..$550.00 – 600.00

Page 136, Thorn Apple
Row 1:
1. Vase, 8½", #816-8 ....$250.00 – 300.00
2. Double bud vase, 5½", #1119 ....$175.00 – 225.00
3. Hanging basket, 7" dia. ....$300.00 – 350.00
4. Triple bud vase, 6", #1120 ....$200.00 – 250.00

Row 2:
1. Bowl vase, 6½", #305-6....................$200.00 – 250.00
2. Vase, 10½", #822-10 ....$300.00 – 350.00
3. Vase, 9", #820-9 ....$275.00 – 325.00

Earlam
Row 1:
1. Vase, 4", #515...................................$325.00 – 350.00
2. Vase, 6", #518...................................$450.00 – 500.00
3. Candlestick, 4", #1080, pair ....$600.00 – 650.00

Row 2:
1. Bowl, 3" x 11½", #218 ....$400.00 – 450.00
2. Vase, 9", #522 ....$800.00 – 900.00
3. Planter, 5½"x 10½", #89 ....$400.00 – 450.00

Page 137, Ixia
Row 1:
1. Hanging basket, 7" ....$250.00 – 300.00
2. Double candlestick, 3", #1127...............$150.00 – 175.00
3. Center bowl, 3½" x 10½", #330-7.........$150.00 – 175.00
4. Candle holder/bud vase, 5", #1128 ....$200.00 – 250.00

Row 2:
1. Vase, 8½", #857-8 ....$175.00 – 225.00
2. Vase, 8½", #858-8 ....$200.00 – 250.00
3. Vase, 10½", #862-10 ....$275.00 – 325.00
4. Vase, 8½", #856-8 ....$200.00 – 250.00

Windsor
Row 1:
1. Center bowl, 3½" x 10½", blue ....$450.00 – 550.00
   rust..$350.00 – 400.00
2. Basket, 4½", #330, blue ....$1,100.00 – 1,200.00
   rust..$900.00 – 1,000.00
3. Center bowl, 3" x 10", blue ....$400.00 – 450.00
   rust..$300.00 – 350.00

Row 2:
1. Vase, 6", #546, blue..........................$400.00 – 450.00
   rust..$300.00 – 350.00
2. Vase, 7", #582, blue..........................$1,750.00 – 2,000.00
   rust..$1,250.00 – 1,500.00
3. Factory lamp base, 7", #551, blue....$1,250.00 – 1,500.00
   rust..$1,000.00 – 1,250.00

Page 138, Moderne
Row 1:
1. Triple candle holder, 6", #1112 ....$275.00 – 350.00
2. Vase, 6½", #299...............................$225.00 – 275.00
3. Vase, 6½", #787...............................$175.00 – 225.00

Row 2:
1. Compote, 6", #297-6 ....$250.00 – 275.00
2. Vase, 8½", #796-8 ....$250.00 – 300.00
3. Vase, 6", #789-6 ....$225.00 – 250.00
4. Compote, 5", #295...............................$250.00 – 275.00

Page 139, Poppy
Row 1:
1. Vase, 6½", #335-6, pink..........................$400.00 – 450.00
   gray/green..$300.00 – 350.00
2. Vase, 5", #642-4, pink..........................$175.00 – 200.00
   gray/green..$150.00 – 175.00
3. Bowl, 12", #336-10, pink ....$275.00 – 300.00
   gray/green..$225.00 – 250.00

Row 2:
1. Bowl, 3½", #642-3, pink..........................$125.00 – 150.00
   gray/green..$100.00 – 125.00
2. Vase, 6", #866-6, pink..........................$175.00 – 200.00
   gray/green..$125.00 – 150.00
3. Vase, 7½", #368-7, pink..........................$225.00 – 250.00
   gray/green..$150.00 – 175.00
4. Vase, 7½", #869-7, pink..........................$225.00 – 250.00
   gray/green..$150.00 – 175.00
5. Vase, 8", #870-8, pink..........................$275.00 – 300.00
   gray/green..$175.00 – 200.00

Row 3:
1. Vase, 9", #872-9, pink.............................$450.00 – 500.00
   gray/green...$300.00 – 325.00
2. Ewer, 18½", #880-18, pink...............$1,000.00 – 1,100.00
   gray/green...$750.00 – 850.00
3. Basket, 12½", #348-12, pink.................$650.00 – 700.00
   gray/green...$500.00 – 550.00
4. Vase, 8", #871-8, pink.........................$400.00 – 450.00
   gray/green...$275.00 – 325.00

Page 140, Primrose
1. Vase, 6½", #761-6, tan ....$150.00 – 175.00
   blue or pink...$175.00 – 200.00
2. Vase, 7", #760-6, tan ....$150.00 – 175.00
   blue or pink...$175.00 – 200.00

Page 141, Baneda
Row 1:
1. Center bowl, 3½" x 10", #233, green .....$600.00 – 700.00
   pink ....$450.00 – 525.00
2. Vase, 4½", #603, green..........................$625.00 – 675.00
   pink ....$525.00 – 625.00
3. Center bowl, 3" x 11", #234, green ....$700.00 – 800.00
   pink ....$550.00 – 625.00

Row 2:
1. Vase, 5", #235, green............................$750.00 – 825.00
   pink ....$650.00 – 725.00
2. Candle holder, 5½", #1087, pair, green ..$750.00 – 825.00
   pink ....$600.00 – 675.00
3. Vase, 7", #606, green............................$750.00 – 825.00
   pink ....$625.00 – 700.00
4. Vase, 6", #602, green............................$650.00 – 700.00
   pink ....$525.00 – 575.00
5. Vase, 4", #587, green............................$475.00 – 525.00
   pink ....$400.00 – 450.00

Row 3:
1. Vase, 7", #592, green............................$725.00 – 800.00
   pink ....$600.00 – 675.00
2. Vase, 7", #610, green............................$725.00 – 800.00
   pink ....$600.00 – 675.00
3. Vase, 9", #594, green.........................$1,000.00 – 1,100.00
   pink ....$850.00 – 950.00
4. Vase, 8", #595, green.........................$1,200.00 – 1,400.00
   pink ....$1,000.00 – 1,200.00

Row 4:
1. Vase, 10", #597, green.......................$1,800.00 – 2,000.00
   pink ....$1,600.00 – 1,800.00
2. Vase, 12", #598, green.......................$1,800.00 – 2,000.00
   pink ....$1,600.00 – 1, 800.00
3. Vase, 12", #599, green.......................$2,750.00 – 3,250.00
   pink ....$2,000.00 – 2,500.00
4. Vase, 9", #596, green.........................$1,500.00 – 1,750.00
   pink ....$1,250.00 – 1,500.00

Page 142, Teasel
1. Vase, 12", #888-12, dark blue or rust.....$500.00 – 600.00
   light blue or tan......................................$450.00 – 550.00
2. Vase, 10", #887-10, dark blue or rust.....$450.00 – 500.00

light blue or tan......................................$350.00 – 400.00
3. Vase, 6", #881-6, dark blue or rust.........$200.00 – 225.00
   light blue or tan......................................$175.00 – 200.00

Page 143, Blackberry
Row 1:
1. Vase, 6"...$550.00 – 600.00
2. Hanging basket, 4½" x 6½".............$1,000.00 – 1,200.00
3. Basket ....$1,100.00 – 1,300.00

Row 2:
1. Jardiniere, 7".....................................$750.00 – 850.00
2. Jardiniere, 6".....................................$550.00 – 650.00
3. Jardiniere, 4".....................................$400.00 – 450.00

Morning Glory
Row 1:
1. Candlestick, 5", #1102, pair, green.........$750.00 – 850.00
   ivory...$600.00 – 700.00
2. Center bowl, 4½" x 11½", #270, green ..$475.00 – 550.00
   ivory...$350.00 – 375.00
3. Vase, 5", #723, green............................$475.00 – 550.00
   ivory...$350.00 – 375.00

Row 2:
1. Basket, 10½", #340, green ....$1,200.00 – 1,300.00
   ivory...$800.00 – 900.00
2. Vase, 14", #732, green.....................$2,500.00 – 3,000.00
   ivory...$1,500.00 – 1,750.00
3. Pillow vase, 7", #120, green ....$550.00 – 600.00
   ivory...$400.00 – 450.00

Page 144, Dawn
1. Vase, 12", #833-12, pink or yellow ....$600.00 – 700.00
   green...$500.00 – 600.00
2. Bowl, 16", #318-4, pink or yellow...........$275.00 – 325.00
   green...$225.00 – 250.00
   Ewer, 16", #834-16, pink or yellow ....$800.00 – 900.00
   green...$650.00 – 750.00

Page 145, Ivory II
Row 1:
1. Cornucopia, 5½" x 12", #2 ....$75.00 – 95.00
2. Jardiniere, 4", #574-4 ....$40.00 – 50.00
3. Vase, 6½", #274-6 ....$75.00 – 95.00
Row 2:
1. Vase, 7" ....$75.00 – 95.00
2. Candlestick, 5½", #1122-5, pair ....$75.00 – 95.00
3. Ewer, 10½", #941-10 ....$75.00 – 95.00
4. Candlestick, 2½", #1114-2, pair ....$40.00 – 60.00
5. Jardiniere, 6" ....$50.00 – 75.00

   Hanging basket, 7" ....$75.00 – 100.00
   Dog, 6½" ....$500.00 – 600.00
   Nude, 9" ....$2,000.00 – 2,500.00

Page 146, Iris
Row 1:
1. Vase, 6½", #917-6, blue.........................$175.00 – 200.00
   pink or tan..$150.00 – 175.00

2. Basket, 9½", #355-10, blue ....$475.00 – 550.00
    pink or tan ....$425.00 – 475.00
3. Vase, 7½", #920-7, blue ....$200.00 – 225.00
    pink or tan ....$175.00 – 200.00

Row 2:
1. Pillow vase, 8½", #922-8, blue ....$325.00 – 275.00
    pink or tan ....$275.00 – 300.00
2. Center bowl, 3" x 10", #361-8, blue ......$200.00 – 225.00
    pink or tan ....$175.00 – 200.00
3. Vase, 6½", #358-6, blue.......................$325.00 – 375.00
    pink or tan ....$275.00 – 300.00

Row 3:
1. Bowl vase, 3½", #647-3, blue................$125.00 – 150.00
    pink or tan ....$100.00 – 125.00
2. Center bowl, 3½" x 12½", #362-10, blue$225.00 – 250.00
    pink or tan ....$200.00 – 225.00
3. Vase, 5", #915-5, blue..........................$125.00 – 150.00
    pink or tan ....$100.00 – 125.00

Row 4:
1. Vase, 8", #923-8, blue...........................$375.00 – 425.00
    pink or tan ....$300.00 – 350.00
2. Vase, 12½", #928-12, blue.....................$550.00 – 650.00
    pink or tan ....$425.00 – 475.00
3. Vase, 10", #924-9, blue.........................$450.00 – 475.00
    pink or tan ....$350.00 – 400.00

Page 147, Bleeding Heart
Row 1:
1. Hanging basket, 8" diameter,
    #362, blue ....$375.00 – 425.00
    pink or green ....$325.00 – 350.00
2. Bowl vase, 3½", #651-3, blue................$125.00 – 150.00
    pink or green ....$100.00 – 125.00
3. Vase, 8", #969-8, blue...........................$375.00 – 425.00
    pink or green ....$325.00 – 350.00
4. Bowl vase, 4", #377-4, blue...................$125.00 – 150.00
    pink or green ....$100.00 – 125.00
5. Vase, 8½", #968-9, blue.........................$375.00 – 425.00
    pink or green ....$325.00 – 350.00
6. Vase, 6½", #964-6, blue.........................$175.00 – 200.00
    pink or green ....$125.00 – 150.00

Row 2:
1. Candlesticks, 5", #1139-4, pair, blue......$275.00 – 325.00
    pink or green ....$250.00 – 275.00
2. Center bowl, 17", #384-14,
    with frog #40, blue ....$300.00 – 350.00
    pink or green ....$225.00 – 275.00

Row 3:
1. Basket, 9½", #360-10, blue ....$500.00 – 550.00
    pink or green ....$425.00 – 475.00
2. Vase, 15", #976-15, blue....................$900.00 – 1,000.00
    pink or green ....$750.00 – 850.00
3. Plate, 10½", #381-10, blue ....$200.00 – 225.00
    pink or green ....$150.00 – 175.00

Page 148, Columbine
Row 1:
1. Vase, 7½", #17-7, pink...........................$225.00 – 275.00

blue or tan ....$175.00 – 225.00
2. Hanging Basket, 8½", pink ....$375.00 – 425.00
    blue or tan ....$325.00 – 375.00
3. Vase, 8", #151-8, pink..........................$275.00 – 325.00
    blue or tan ....$225.00 – 275.00

Row 2:
1. Bookend planter, 5", #8, pair, pink ....$450.00 – 550.00
    blue or tan ....$350.00 – 400.00
2. Candle holders, 5", #1146-4½, pr., pink ..$225.00 – 250.00
    blue or tan ....$175.00 – 200.00
3. Cornucopia, 5½", #149-6, pink ....$175.00 – 200.00
    blue or tan ....$150.00 – 175.00

Page 149, Fuchsia
Row 1:
1. Vase, 6", #893-6, blue...........................$250.00 – 300.00
    green ....$200.00 – 225.00
    brown/tan ....$175.00 – 200.00
2. Vase, 6", #891-6, blue...........................$250.00 – 300.00
    green ....$200.00 – 225.00
    brown/tan ....$175.00 – 200.00
3. Vase, 6", #892-6, blue...........................$250.00 – 300.00
    green ....$200.00 – 225.00
    brown/tan ....$175.00 – 200.00

Row 2:
1. Candlesticks, 2", #1132, pair, blue ....$175.00 – 200.00
    green ....$150.00 – 175.00
    brown/tan ....$125.00 – 150.00
2. Center bowl, 3½" x 12½", #351-10, blue$300.00 – 350.00
    green ....$225.00 – 275.00
    brown/tan ....$200.00 – 225.00

Row 3:
1. Candlesticks, 5½", #1133-5, pair, blue ..$500.00 – 550.00
    green ....$400.00 – 450.00
    brown/tan ....$300.00 – 350.00
2. Center Bowl, 4" x 15½", #353-14, blue..$375.00 – 425.00
    green ....$300.00 – 350.00
    brown/tan ....$275.00 – 325.00
3. Frog, #37, blue.....................................$250.00 – 300.00
    green ....$225.00 – 250.00
    brown/tan ....$200.00 – 225.00

Row 4:
1. Vase, 8", #897-8, blue...........................$450.00 – 500.00
    green ....$350.00 – 400.00
    brown/tan ....$300.00 – 350.00
2. Vase, 8½", #896-8, blue.........................$450.00 – 500.00
    green ....$350.00 – 400.00
    brown/tan ....$300.00 – 350.00
3. Vase, 8", #898-8, blue...........................$475.00 – 525.00
    green ....$375.00 – 425.00
    brown/tan ....$325.00 – 375.00

Page 150, Cosmos
Row 1:
1. Hanging basket, 7", #361, blue ....$400.00 – 425.00
    green ....$375.00 – 425.00
    tan ....$300.00 – 350.00

2. Vase, 8", #950-8, blue..............................$400.00 – 425.00
   green ....$375.00 – 425.00
   tan ....$300.00 – 350.00
3. Vase, 5", #945-5, blue..............................$200.00 – 225.00
   green ....$175.00 – 200.00
   tan ....$150.00 – 175.00
4. Vase, 4", #375-4, blue..............................$225.00 – 250.00
   green ....$200.00 – 225.00
   tan ....$175.00 – 200.00
4. Vase, 6½", #946, blue..............................$200.00 – 250.00
   green ....$175.00 – 200.00
   tan ....$150.00 – 175.00
5. Vase, 12½", #956-12, blue.....................$650.00 – 750.00
   green ....$600.00 – 650.00
   tan ....$500.00 – 550.00

Row 2:
1. Vase, 4", #134-4, blue..............................$175.00 – 200.00
   green ....$150.00 – 175.00
   tan ....$125.00 – 150.00
2. Center bowl, 15½", #374-14, blue.........$325.00 – 375.00
   green ....$300.00 – 350.00
   tan ....$250.00 – 300.00
3. Flower frog, 3½", #39, blue ....$200.00 – 250.00
   green ....$175.00 – 225.00
   tan ....$150.00 – 175.00

Page 151, White Rose
Row 1:
1. Vase, 4", #978-4 ....$80.00 – 90.00
2. Vase, 5", #980-6 ....$90.00 – 110.00
3. Basket, 7½", #362-8 ....$200.00 – 250.00
4. Vase, 6", #979-6 ....$110.00 – 135.00
5. Candlestick, 4½", #1142-4½, pair ....$125.00 – 150.00

Row 2:
1. Vase, 7", #388-7 ....$150.00 – 200.00
2. Vase, 8", #984-8 ....$150.00 – 200.00
3. Vase, 8½", #985-8 ....$150.00 – 200.00

Row 3:
1. Double bud vase, 4½", #148 ....$85.00 – 95.00
2. Console/frog, 16½", #393-12, frog #41..$150.00 – 200.00
3. Double candle holder, 4", #1143, pair ...$200.00 – 250.00

Row 4:
1. Vase, 12½", #991-12 ....$250.00 – 300.00
2. Vase, 15½", #992-15 ....$300.00 – 400.00
3. Vase, 9", #987-9 ....$150.00 – 200.00

Page 152, Bittersweet
Row 1:
1. Basket, 8½", #809-8 ....$200.00 – 250.00
2. Vase, 6", #881-6 ....$100.00 – 125.00
3. Bowl vase, 7", #842-7............................$200.00 – 250.00

Row 2:
1. Planter, 10½", #828-10 ....$150.00 – 175.00
2. Planter, 11½", #827-8 ....$150.00 – 175.00
3. Cornucopia, 4½", #857-4 ....$100.00 – 125.00

Row 3:
1. Candlesticks, 3", #851-3, pair ....$150.00 – 175.00
2. Center bowl, 12½", #829-12...................$175.00 – 200.00
3. Double vase, 4", #858...........................$150.00 – 175.00

Row 4:
1. Vase, 7", #874-7 ....$125.00 – 150.00
2. Vase, 10", #885-10 ....$200.00 – 225.00
3. Vase, 15½", #888-16 ....$450.00 – 500.00
4. Vase, 8", #884-8 ....$150.00 – 175.00

Page 153, Foxglove
Row 1:
1. Tray, 8½", #419, green/pink ....$200.00 – 225.00
   blue ....$175.00 – 200.00
   pink ....$150.00 – 175.00
2. Hanging basket, 6½", #466, green/pink .$350.00 – 400.00
   blue ....$325.00 – 375.00
   pink ....$300.00 – 350.00
3. Cornucopia, 6", #166-6, green/pink ....$200.00 – 225.00
   blue ....$175.00 – 200.00
   pink ....$150.00 – 175.00

Row 2:
1. Tray, 15" wide, #424, green/pink ....$350.00 – 400.00
   blue ....$300.00 – 350.00
   pink ....$250.00 – 300.00
2. Flower frog, 4", #46, green/pink ....$150.00 – 175.00
   blue ....$125.00 – 150.00
   pink ....$125.00 – 150.00
3. Tray, 11", #420, green/pink ....$250.00 – 300.00
   blue ....$225.00 – 275.00
   pink ....$200.00 – 250.00

Row 3:
1. Vase, 12½", #52-12, green/pink ....$450.00 – 500.00
   blue ....$400.00 – 450.00
   pink ....$350.00 – 400.00
2. Vase, 14", #53-14, green/pink ....$500.00 – 550.00
   blue ....$450.00 – 500.00
   pink ....$400.00 – 450.00
3. Vase, 10", #51-10, green/pink ....$350.00 – 400.00
   blue ....$300.00 – 350.00
   pink ....$250.00 – 300.00
4. Vase, 8½", #47-8, green/pink ....$275.00 – 325.00
   blue ....$250.00 – 300.00
   pink ....$225.00 – 275.00

Page 154, Peony
Row 1:
1. Bookend, 5½", #11, pair. ....$200.00 – 250.00
2. Conch shell, 9½", #436.........................$110.00 – 135.00
3. Tray, 8" ....$75.00 – 100.00

Row 2:
1. Planter, 10", #387-8 ....$85.00 – 95.00
2. Bowl, 11", #430-10 ....$100.00 – 125.00

Row 3:
1. Double candle holder, 5", #115-3, pair...$200.00 – 250.00
2. Mug, 3½", #2-3½....................................$100.00 – 125.00
3. Pitcher, 7½", #1326-7½ ....$275.00 – 325.00
4. Frog, 4", #47 ....$85.00 – 95.00

Row 4:
1. Vase, 8", #169-8 ....$125.00 – 150.00
2. Basket, 11", #379-12 ....$250.00 – 275.00
3. Vase, 14", #68-14 ....$300.00 – 350.00

Page 155, Magnolia
Row 1:
1. Planter, 8½", #388-6 ....$85.00 – 95.00
2. Planter, 6", #183-6 ....$90.00 – 110.00
3. Candlestick, 5", #1157-4½, pair ....$120.00 – 150.00
4. Candlestick, 2½", #1156-2½, pair ....$100.00 – 125.00

Row 2:
1. Ashtray, 7", #28.................................$100.00 – 125.00
2. Center bowl, 14½", #5-10.....................$125.00 – 175.00
3. Cornucopia, 6", #184-6 ....$85.00 – 95.00

Row 3:
1. Vase, 6", #180-6 ....$95.00 – 110.00
2. Flower frog, 5½", #182-5 ....$95.00 – 110.00
3. Conch shell, 6½", #453-6 ....$95.00 – 110.00
4. Vase, 6", #88-6 ....$95.00 – 110.00

Row 4:
1. Basket, 12", #386-12 ....$275.00 – 325.00
2. Ewer, 10", #14-10 ....$175.00 – 200.00
3. Vase, 8", #91-8 ....$125.00 – 150.00

Page 156, Water Lily
1. Vase, 9", #78-9, rose with green.............$350.00 – 400.00
   blue ....$325.00 – 350.00
   brown ....$300.00 – 325.00
2. Candlesticks, 5", #1155-4½, pair,
   rose with green ....$225.00 – 250.00
   blue ....$200.00 – 225.00
   brown ....$180.00 – 190.00
3. Hanging basket, 9", #468,
   rose with green ....$375.00 – 425.00
   blue ....$350.00 – 375.00
   brown ....$325.00 – 350.00
4. Frog, 4½", #48, rose with green ....$175.00 – 200.00
   blue ....$160.00 – 175.00
   brown with green ....$140.00 – 165.00

Page 157, Freesia
Row 1:
1. Flowerpot/saucer, 5½", #670-5, green ...$225.00 – 250.00
   blue ....$200.00 – 225.00
   tangerine ....$185.00 – 210.00
2. Basket, 7", #390-7, green ....$275.00 – 300.00
   blue ....$250.00 – 275.00
   tangerine ....$225.00 – 250.00
3. Jardiniere, 4", #669-4, green ....$150.00 – 175.00
   blue ....$125.00 – 150.00
   tangerine ....$100.00 – 125.00

Row 2:
1. Center bowl, 8½", #464-6, green ....$150.00 – 175.00
   blue ....$125.00 – 150.00
   tangerine ....$100.00 – 125.00

2. Bowl, 11", #465-8, green ....$175.00 – 200.00
   blue ....$150.00 – 175.00
   tangerine ....$125.00 – 150.00

Row 3:
1. Candle holders, 2",#1160-2, pair, green.$140.00 – 160.00
   blue ....$120.00 – 140.00
   tangerine ....$90.00 – 110.00
2. Center bowl, 16½", #469-14, green ....$325.00 – 350.00
   blue ....$275.00 – 300.00
   tangerine ....$250.00 – 275.00

Row 4:
1. Vase, 5", #463-5, green ....$225.00 – 250.00
   blue ....$200.00 – 225.00
   tangerine ....$185.00 – 210.00
2. Vase, 7", #119-7, green ....$150.00 – 175.00
   blue ....$125.00 – 150.00
   tangerine ....$100.00 – 125.00
3. Window box, 10½", #1392-8, green.......$200.00 – 225.00
   blue ....$175.00 – 200.00
   tangerine ....$150.00 – 175.00

Row 5:
1. Vase, 8", #212-8, green ....$225.00 – 250.00
   blue ....$200.00 – 225.00
   tangerine ....$175.00 – 200.00
2. Vase, 9½", #123-9, green ....$250.00 – 275.00
   blue ....$225.00 – 250.00
   tangerine ....$200.00 – 225.00
3. Vase, 10½", #125-10, green ....$275.00 – 300.00
   blue ....$250.00 – 275.00
   tangerine ....$225.00 – 250.00
4. Vase, 9", #124-9, green ....$275.00 – 300.00
   blue ....$250.00 – 275.00
   tangerine ....$225.00 – 250.00

Page 158, Rozane Pattern
1. Vase, 12", #10-12 ....$400.00 – 450.00
2. Bowl, 7½", #8-8, with ornament, 5",
   #1, set .... $350.00 – 400.00
3. Vase, 8½", #5-8 ....$225.00 – 275.00

Page 159, Zephyr Lily
Row 1:
1. Fan vase, 6½", #205-6, blue..................$175.00 – 200.00
   brown ....$150.00 – 175.00
   green ....$125.00 – 150.00
2. Hanging basket, 7½", blue ....$350.00 – 400.00
   brown ....$300.00 – 350.00
   green ....$275.00 – 300.00
3. Pillow vase, 7", #206-7, blue ....$225.00 – 275.00
   brown ....$200.00 – 225.00
   green ....$175.00 – 200.00

Row 2:
1. Candle holders, 2", #1162-2, pair, blue ..$150.00 – 175.00
   brown ....$125.00 – 150.00
   green ....$100.00 – 175.00
2. Center bowl, 16½", #479-14, blue..........$250.00 – 275.00
   brown ....$225.00 – 250.00
   green ....$200.00 – 225.00

3. Bud vase, 7½", #201-7, blue ....$175.00 – 200.00
   brown ....$150.00 – 175.00
   green ....$125.00 – 150.00

Row 3:
1. Vase, 8½", #133-8, blue.........................$175.00 – 200.00
   brown ....$150.00 – 175.00
   green ....$125.00 – 150.00
2. Tray, 14½", blue ....$250.00 – 275.00
   brown ....$225.00 – 250.00
   green ....$200.00 – 225.00
3. Cornucopia, 8½", #204-8, blue ....$175.00 – 200.00
   brown ....$150.00 – 175.00
   green ....$125.00 – 150.00

Row 4:
1. Vase, 9½", #135-9, blue.........................$250.00 – 275.00
   brown ....$225.00 – 250.00
   green ....$200.00 – 225.00
2. Vase, 12", #139-12, blue........................$350.00 – 400.00
   brown ....$300.00 – 350.00
   green ....$275.00 – 300.00
3. Vase, 12½", #140-12, blue......................$375.00 – 425.00
   brown ....$325.00 – 375.00
   green ....$300.00 – 325.00
4. Vase, 8½", #202-8, blue.........................$250.00 – 275.00
   brown ....$225.00 – 250.00
   green ....$200.00 – 225.00

Page 160, Clematis
Row 1:
1. Center bowl, 14", #458-10, blue.............$200.00 – 250.00
   green or brown................................$175.00 – 200.00
2. Candle holder, 2½", #1158-2, pair, blue.$110.00 – 130.00
   green or brown................................$95.00 – 110.00
3. Center bowl, 9", #456-6, blue................$150.00 – 175.00
   green or brown................................$125.00 – 150.00

Row 2:
1. Flower arranger, 5½", #192-5, blue ....$100.00 – 125.00
   green or brown................................$90.00 – 110.00
2. Flowerpot with saucer, 5½",
   #668-5, blue...$175.00 – 200.00
   green or brown................................$150.00 – 175.00
3. Vase, 6", #103-6, blue..........................$100.00 – 125.00
   green or brown................................$90.00 – 110.00
4. Flower frog, 4½", #50, blue ....$95.00 – 110.00
   green or brown................................$80.00 – 95.00
5. Vase, 6½", #102-6, blue........................$110.00 – 130.00
   green or brown................................$95.00 – 110.00

Page 161, Snowberry
Row 1:
1. Vase, 6", #IRB-6, blue or pink ....$200.00 – 225.00
   green ....$150.00 – 175.00
2. Pillow vase, 6½", #1FH-6, blue or pink ..$150.00 – 175.00
   green ....$100.00 – 125.00
3. Flowerpot, 5½", #1PS-5, blue or pink ....$225.00 – 250.00
   green ....$200.00 – 225.00

Row 2:
1. Candlesticks, 4½", #1CS-2, pair

blue or pink ....$175.00 – 225.00
   green ....$150.00 – 175.00
2. Center bowl, 11", #1BL-8, blue or pink ..$150.00 – 175.00
   green ....$125.00 – 150.00

Row 3:
1. Vase, 6", #1V-6, blue or pink ....$90.00 – 110.00
   green ....$70.00 – 85.00
2. Tray, 14", #1BL-12, blue or pink ....$250.00 – 275.00
   green ....$200.00 – 225.00
3. Vase, 7½", #1V2-7, blue or pink ....$110.00 – 130.00
   green ....$85.00 – 100.00

Row 4:
1. Vase, 12½", #1V1-12, blue or pink ....$300.00 – 350.00
   green ....$275.00 – 300.00
2. Ewer, 16", #1TK-15, blue or pink...........$600.00 – 700.00
   green ....$525.00 – 575.00
3. Basket, 12½", #1BK-12, blue or pink .....$350.00 – 375.00
   green ....$275.00 – 325.00
4. Vase, 8½", #1UR-8, blue or pink ....$225.00 – 250.00
   green ....$175.00 – 200.00

Page 162, Apple Blossom
Row 1:
1. Bowl, 2½" x 6½", #326-6, blue..............$175.00 – 200.00
   pink or green.................................$150.00 – 175.00
2. Bowl vase, 6", #342-6, blue...................$325.00 – 375.00
   pink or green.................................$275.00 – 325.00
3. Window box, 2½" x 10½",
   #368-8, blue...$200.00 – 225.00
   pink or green.................................$175.00 – 200.00

Row 2:
1. Vase, 10", #388-10, blue........................$350.00 – 450.00
   pink or green.................................$300.00 – 350.00
2. Vase, 15½", #392-15, blue....................$900.00 – 1,000.00
   pink or green.................................$800.00 – 900.00
3. Vase, 12½", #390-12, blue....................$450.00 – 500.00
   pink or green.................................$400.00 – 450.00

Page 163, Gardenia
Row 1:
1. Hanging basket, 6", #661 ....$300.00 – 350.00
2. Bowl, 5", #641-5 ....$125.00 – 150.00
3. Window box, 3" x 8½", #658-8 ....$100.00 – 125.00
4. Vase, 8", #683-8 ....$150.00 – 175.00

Row 2:
1. Vase, 10", #685-10 ....$175.00 – 225.00
2. Tray, 15", #631-14 ....$200.00 – 250.00
3. Vase, 10½", #686-10 ....$225.00 – 250.00

Row 3:
1. Basket, 12", #610-12 ....$350.00 – 400.00
2. Vase, 12", #687-12 ....$275.00 – 300.00
3. Vase, 14½", #689-14 ....$375.00 – 425.00

Page 164, Mayfair
1. Jardiniere, 7½", #90-4 ....$50.00 – 75.00
2. Pitcher, 5", #1101-5 ....$75.00 – 85.00

3. Pitcher, 5", #1102-5 ....$75.00 – 85.00
4. Cornucopia, 3" x 6½", #1013-6 ....$60.00 – 75.00

Row 1:
  1. Jardiniere, 4", #1109-4 ....$60.00 – 75.00
  2. Planter, 3½" x 8½", #113-8......................$70.00 – 85.00

Row 2:
  1. Flowerpot, 4½", #71-4 ....$70.00 – 85.00
  2. Vase, 7", #1104-9 ....$90.00 – 100.00
  3. Teapot, 5", #1121 ....$125.00 – 150.00

Row 3:
  1. Candle holder, 4½", #115-1, pair...............$50.00 – 60.00
  2. Bowl, 7" ....$40.00 – 50.00
  3. Bowl, 10", #1119-9 ....$60.00 – 70.00
  4. Vase, 12½", #1106-12 ....$90.00 – 110.00

Page 165, Bushberry
Row 1:
  1. Double cornucopia, 6", #155-8, blue .....$200.00 – 225.00
     green ....$175.00 – 200.00
     orange ....$150.00 – 175.00
  2. Candle holder, 2", #1447-2CS, pair, blue $175.00 – 200.00
     green ....$150.00 – 175.00
     orange ....$125.00 – 150.00
  3. Hanging basket, 7", blue ....$450.00 – 500.00
     green ....$400.00 – 450.00
     orange ....$375.00 – 425.00
  4. Vase, 4", #28-4, blue..............................$100.00 – 125.00
     green ....$75.00 – 85.00
     orange ....$65.00 – 75.00
  5. Vase, 7", #32-7, blue...............................$175.00 – 200.00
     green ....$150.00 – 175.00
     orange ....$125.00 – 150.00

Row 2:
  1. Double bud vase, 4½", #158-4½, blue...$175.00 – 200.00
     green ....$150.00 – 175.00
     orange ....$125.00 – 150.00
  2. Center bowl, 13", #385-10, blue............$175.00 – 200.00
     green ....$150.00 – 175.00
     orange ....$125.00 – 150.00
  3. Window box, 6½", #383-6, blue ....$150.00 – 175.00
     green ....$125.00 – 150.00
     orange ....$100.00 – 125.00

Row 3:
  1. Ice-lip pitcher, 8½", #1325, blue............$550.00 – 650.00
     green ....$450.00 – 475.00
     orange ....$375.00 – 425.00
  2. Mug, 3½", #1-3½, blue ....$200.00 – 225.00
     green ....$175.00 – 200.00
     orange ....$150.00 – 175.00
  3. Vase, 6", #156-6, blue.............................$150.00 – 175.00
     green ....$125.00 – 150.00
     orange ....$100.00 – 125.00
  4. Bud vase, 7½", #152-7, blue ....$175.00 – 200.00
     green ....$150.00 – 175.00
     orange ....$125.00 – 150.00
  5. Bowl vase, 6", #411-6, blue....................$300.00 – 350.00
     green ....$250.00 – 275.00
     orange ....$225.00 – 250.00

Row 4:
  1. Vase, 8", #34-8, blue.............................$250.00 – 275.00
     green ....$225.00 – 250.00
     orange ....$200.00 – 225.00
  2. Vase, 12½", #38-12, blue......................$450.00 – 500.00
     green ....$400.00 – 450.00
     orange ....$375.00 – 425.00
  3. Vase, 14½", #39-14, blue......................$550.00 – 650.00
     green ....$475.00 – 550.00
     orange ....$400.00 – 475.00
  4. Vase, 8", #157-8, blue...........................$250.00 – 275.00
     green ....$225.00 – 250.00
     orange ....$200.00 – 225.00

Page 166, Florane
Row 1:
  1. Bowl, 10" ....$30.00 – 35.00
  2. Bowl, 9"...$50.00 – 60.00

Row 2:
  1. Bowl, 6" ....$20.00 – 25.00
  2. Bowl, 12"...$65.00 – 75.00
  3. Bowl, 8" ....$20.00 – 25.00

Row 3:
  1. Vase, 6" ....$30.00 – 35.00
  2. Bud vase, 7" ....$30.00 – 35.00
  3. Vase, 7" ....$40.00 – 45.00

Row 4:
  1. Vase, 9" ....$75.00 – 90.00
  2. Vase, 11" ....$75.00 – 100.00
  3. Vase, 14" ....$90.00 – 115.00

Row 1:
  1. Planter box, 6" ....$25.00 – 30.00
  2. Bowl, 7" ....$20.00 – 25.00
  3. Planter, 6" ....$25.00 – 30.00

Row 2:
  1. Planter, 10" ....$45.00 – 50.00
  2. Planter, 4" ....$20.00 – 25.00
  3. Planter, 8" ....$35.00 – 40.00

Row 3:
  1. Pot, 4" ....$20.00 – 25.00
  2. Pot, 5" ....$25.00 – 30.00
  3. Pot, 6" ....$35.00 – 40.00
  4. Bowl, 10" ....$25.00 – 30.00

Row 4:
  1. Sand jar, 12" ....$100.00 – 135.00
  2. Jar, 10" ....$100.00 – 125.00
  3. Jar, 8" ....$90.00 – 115.00

Page 167, Wincraft
  1. Vase, 7", #274-7 ....$225.00 – 250.00
  2. Basket, 12", #210-12 ....$500.00 – 600.00

Row 1:
  1. Cornucopia, 9" x 5", #221-8..................$150.00 – 175.00

2. Dealer sign, 4½" x 8" ....$5,000.00 – 6,000.00
3. Mug, 4½" ....$100.00 – 125.00

Row 2:
1. Center bowl, 4" x 13½", #227-10 ....$150.00 – 175.00
2. Bookends, 6½", #259, pair ....$175.00 – 225.00

Row 3:
1. Vase, 16", #288-15 ....$375.00 – 425.00
2. Ewer, 19", #218-18 ....$650.00 – 750.00

Page 168, Artwood
Row 1:
1. 3-pc. Planter set, side section, 4", #1050;
   center section, 6", #1051-6 ....$110.00 – 125.00
2. Planter, 6½" x 8½", #1054-8½.....................$85.00 – 95.00

Row 2:
1. Planter, 7" x 9½", #1055-9.........................$85.00 – 95.00
2. Vase, 8", #1057-8 ....$85.00 – 95.00
3. Planter, 6½" x 10½", #1056-10...................$85.00 – 95.00

Page 169, Ming Tree
Row 1:
1. Hanging basket, 6" ....$225.00 – 250.00
2. Bowl, 4" x 11½", #526-9 ....$95.00 – 110.00
3. Planter, 4" x 8½" ....$95.00 – 110.00
4. Window box, 4" x 11", #569-10 ....$125.00 – 150.00

Row 2:
1. Bookend, 5½", #559, pair ....$200.00 – 235.00
2. Vase, 6½", #572-6 ....$95.00 – 110.00
3. Ashtray, 6", #599..................................$75.00 – 85.00
4. Conch shell, 8½", #563..........................$90.00 – 110.00
5. Vase, 10½", #583-10 ....$175.00 – 200.00

Row 3:
1. Vase, 12½", #584-12 ....$225.00 – 250.00
2. Vase, 14½", #585-14 ....$400.00 – 450.00
3. Basket, 14½", #510-14 ....$275.00 – 300.00
4. Basket, 13", #509-12 ....$275.00 – 300.00

Page 171, Raymor
Row 1:
1. Gravy boat, 9½", #190...........................$30.00 – 35.00
2. Salad bowl, 11½", #161..........................$35.00 – 40.00
3. Glass tumblers, 4½" ....$35.00 – 40.00

Row 2:
1. Individual casserole, 7½", #199.................$40.00 – 45.00
2. Individual corn server, 12½", #162 ....$45.00 – 50.00
3. Shirred egg, 10", #200...........................$40.00 – 45.00

Row 3:
1. Individual covered ramekin, 6½", #156 ......$35.00 – 40.00
2. Divided vegetable bowl, 13", #165............$55.00 – 65.00
3. Covered butter, 7½", #181......................$75.00 – 100.00

Row 4:
1. Handled coffee tumbler, 4" ....$40.00 – 50.00

2. Condiment set:
   Tray, 8½" ....$40.00 – 50.00
   Cruet, 5½" ....$65.00 – 75.00
   Mustard, 3½" ....$50.00 – 60.00
   Salt and pepper, 3½" ....$30.00 – 35.00
3. Large casserole, 13½" ....$85.00 – 95.00
   Add $25.00 for lid

Row 5:
1. Vegetable, 9", #160................................$30.00 – 40.00
2. Water pitcher, 10", #189 ....$100.00 – 150.00
3. Medium casserole, 11", #183 ....$75.00 – 85.00

Page 172, Raymor Modern Artware
Row 1:
1. Vase, 6½" ....$500.00 – 600.00
2. Bowl, 3" x 7", #41-6 ....$300.00 – 350.00

Row 2:
1. Ashtray, 3½"..$25.00 – 35.00
2. Capri, 10", #533-10 ....$40.00 – 45.00
3. Capri square dish, 4" x 2", #552 ....$25.00 – 35.00
4. Ashtray, 3½"..$25.00 – 35.00

Row 3:
1. Wall pocket, 10½", #711 ....$250.00 – 300.00
2. Capri vase, 12½", #593-12 ....$150.00 – 175.00
3. Star, 2" x 10", #713...............................$75.00 – 100.00

Row 4:
1. Teapot, 6½" ....$125.00 – 150.00
2. Cookie jar, 10", #20...............................$200.00 – 225.00
3. Mixing bowl, 5½", #11-8.........................$40.00 – 45.00
1. Mixing bowl, 9", #11-8............................$55.00 – 65.00
2. Mixing bowl, 8", #10..............................$45.00 – 55.00
3. Mixing bowl, 7", #10-6...........................$35.00 – 45.00

Page 173, Silhouette
Row 1:
1. Box, 4½", #740 ....$150.00 – 175.00
2. Double planter, 5½", #757-9...................$125.00 – 150.00
3. Ewer, 6½", #716-6 ....$100.00 – 125.00

Row 2:
1. Vase, 6", #781-6 ....$90.00 – 110.00
2. Vase, 8", #784-8 ....$100.00 – 125.00
3. Vase, 14", #789-14 ....$350.00 – 400.00
4. Vase, 10", #787-10, with nude................$750.00 – 850.00
5. Vase, 6", #780-6 ....$90.00 – 110.00

Lotus
1. Planter, 3½" x 4", #L9-4.........................$100.00 – 125.00
2. Pillow vase, 10½", #L4-10 ....$275.00 – 325.00
3. Bowl, 3" x 9", #L6-9 ....$150.00 – 175.00

Page 174, Mock Orange
Row 1:
1. Window box, 8½" x 4½", #956-8 ....$100.00 – 125.00
2. Planter, 3½" x 9", #931-8.......................$125.00 – 150.00
3. Planter, 4" x 10½", #932 ....$125.00 – 150.00

Row 2:
1. Vase, 8½", #973-8 ....$150.00 – 175.00
2. Vase, 13", #985-12 ....$350.00 – 450.00
3. Pillow vase, 7", #930-8 ....$150.00 – 175.00

Page 175, Royal Capri
1. Leaf, 2" x 10½", #533-10 ....$200.00 –225.00
2. Vase, 9", #583-9 ....$250.00 – 275.00

Capri
Row 1:
1. Leaf, 16", #532-16 ....$35.00 – 45.00
2. Leaf, 15", #531-14 ....$35.00 – 45.00

Row 2:
1. Window box, 3" x 10", #569-10 ....$45.00 – 55.00
2. Planter, 5" x 10½", #C-1010-10 ......$45.00 – 55.00

Row 3:
1. Bowl, 9", #529-9 ....$20.00 – 30.00
2. Ashtray, 9", #598-9 ....$40.00 – 50.00
3. Bowl, 7", #527-7 ....$20.00 – 30.00

Row 4:
1. Planter, 7", #558 ....$85.00 – 95.00
2. Shell, 13½", #C-1120 ....$50.00 – 60.00
3. Vase, 9", #582-9 ....$50.00 – 60.00

Page 176, Assorted Items
Row 1:
1. Leaf dish, 10½", #533-10 ....$45.00 – 50.00
2. Basket, 7", #508-7 ....$150.00 – 175.00

Row 2:
1. Capri bowl, 7", #527-7 ....$30.00 – 40.00
2. Capri cornucopia, 6", #556-6 ....$85.00 – 95.00
3. Crystal Green bowl, 7", #357-6 ......$100.00 – 125.00

Row 3:
1. Hyde Park ashtray, 8½", #1900 ....$30.00 – 40.00
2. Burmese candlesticks, 3", #75-B, pair ...$40.00 – 50.00
3. Burmese planter, 10", #908-10 ....$50.00 – 60.00
Row 4:
1. Ashtray, 13", #599-13 ....$50.00 – 60.00
2. Ashtray, 13", #204-13 ....$50.00 – 60.00

Page 177, Assorted Items
Row 1:
1. Ashtray, 8½", #1925 ....$30.00 – 40.00
2. Ashtray, 5½", #1915 ....$30.00 – 40.00
3. Ashtray, #1950 ....$30.00 – 40.00

Row 2:
1. Tray, 8" ....$40.00 – 50.00
2. Planter, 4", #1510 ....$40.00 – 45.00
3. Section of 5-part relish, 9½" x 5½", #1507 $15.00 – 20.00

Pasadena
1. Planter, 9" x 3½", #L-17 ....$40.00 – 45.00
2. Planter, 6½" x 5½", #L-38 ....$60.00 – 70.00

3. Planter, 3½" x 10½", #L-35 ....$65.00 – 75.00
Add $5.00 for brass frame

Kettle and Skillet Set
Row 1:
1. Bowl, 2" x 5", #1797 ....$30.00 – 40.00
2. Skillet/ashtray, 6½", #1799 ....$35.00 – 45.00
3. Pot, #1798 ....$30.00 – 40.00

Row 2:
1. Bowl, 2" x 5", #1797 ....$40.00 – 50.00
2. Skillet/ashtray, 6½", #1799 ....$45.00 – 55.00
3. Pot, #1798, in blue ....$40.00 – 50.00
4. Box ....$50.00 – 75.00

Page 178, Wall Pockets
Row 1:
1. Chloron Boy, 9½" ....$3,500.00 – 4,500.00
2. Chloron Corner Vase, 17" ....$2,000.00 – 2,500.00
3. Chloron Girl, 9½" ....$3,500.00 – 4,500.00

Row 2:
1. Chloron, 11½" ....$1,500.00 – 1,750.00
2. Chloron Sconce, 12½" x 12" ....$5,500.00 – 6,500.00
3. Chloron, 11" ....$1,000.00 – 1,100.00

Row 3:
1. Antique Matt Green, 10" ....$600.00 – 700.00
2. Matt Green, 11" ....$400.00 – 500.00

Page 179, Wall Pockets, Sconces
Row 1:
1. Chloron Sconce, 17" ....$3,500.00 – 4,000.00
2. Chloron Sconce, 12" ....$2,500.00 – 3,000.00
3. Chloron Sconce, 17" ....$6,000.00 – 7,000.00

Row 2:
1. Matt Green wall pocket, 15" ....$850.00 – 950.00
2. Chloron letter receiver, 15½" .....$4,000.00 – 5,000.00
3. Chloron Sconce, 10" ....$2,500.00 – 3,000.00

Row 3:
1. Chloron/Nude, 8½" ....$3,000.00 – 3,500.00
2. Chloron wall pocket, 8" ....$3,000.00 – 3,500.00

Page 180, Wall Pockets
Top center:
Landscape, 2½" ....$500.00 – 600.00

Row 1:
1. Persian, 11" ....$500.00 – 600.00
2. Ceramic Design, 17" ....$800.00 – 900.00
3. Ceramic Design, 10" ....$400.00 – 450.00

Row 2:
1. Pink Tint, 14½" ....$500.00 – 600.00
2. Persian, 13½" ....$2,000.00 – 2,500.00
3. Green Tint, 14½" ....$450.00 – 550.00

Row 3:
1. Yellow Tint, 10" ....$200.00 – 225.00

2. Ceramic Design, 11" ....$400.00 – 450.00
3. Ivory I, 10" ....$250.00 – 300.00
4. Green Tint, 10" ....$250.00 – 300.00

Page 181, Wall Pockets, Carnelian I
Row 1:
1. 9½" ....$250.00 – 300.00
2. 8" ....$250.00 – 300.00
3. 8" ....$250.00 – 300.00
4. 8" ....$250.00 – 300.00

Carnelian II
Row 2:
1. 8" ....$550.00 – 650.00
2. 8" ....$550.00 – 650.00
3. 8" ....$550.00 – 650.00
4. 8" ....$550.00 – 650.00

Row 3:
1. Azurine, Orchid, and Turquoise, 10" ....$175.00 – 225.00
2. Rosecraft Blue, 10½" ....$175.00 – 225.00
3. Rosecraft Black, 9" ....$175.00 – 225.00
4. Rosecraft Yellow, 10" ....$175.00 – 225.00

Row 4:
1. Mostique, 9½" ....$550.00 – 600.00
2. Volpato, 8½" ....$650.00 – 750.00
3. Velmoss Scroll, 11" ....$375.00 – 450.00
4. Rozane 1917, 7½" ....$400.00 – 475.00

Page 182, Wall Pockets
Row 1:
1. Dogwood I, 9" ....$450.00 – 500.00
2. Dogwood I, 15" ....$800.00 – 900.00
3. Donatello, 11½" ....$250.00 – 275.00
4. Donatello, 9" ....$175.00 – 200.00

Row 2:
1. Corinthian, 12" ....$350.00 – 400.00
2. Vista, 9½" ....$1,100.00 – 1,300.00
3. Ivory Florentine, 8½", #1238.................$600.00 – 700.00
4. Florentine, 12½" ....$300.00 – 350.00

Row 3:
1. Savona, 8" ....$750.00 – 850.00
2. Imperial I, 10" ....$300.00 – 350.00
3. Imperial I, 10" ....$300.00 – 350.00
4. Dogwood II, 9½" ....$350.00 – 400.00

Row 4:
1. Lombardy, 8" ....$300.00 – 350.00
2. Lombardy, 8" ....$300.00 – 350.00
3. Rosecraft Vintage, 9" ....$400.00 – 450.00
4. Rosecraft Vintage, 9" ....$450.00 – 500.00

Page 183, Wall Pockets
Row 1:
1. Florane, 9" ....$175.00 – 225.00
2. Florane, 10½" ....$225.00 – 275.00
3. Rosecraft Hexagon, 8½" ....$450.00 – 500.00

4. La Rose, 12" ....$350.00 – 400.00
5. La Rose, 7½" ....$200.00 – 250.00

Row 2:
1. Futura, 8" ....$800.00 – 900.00
2. Tuscany, 7" ....$375.00 – 450.00
3. Rosecraft Hexagon, 8½"................$1,000.00 – 1,250.00
4. Tuscany, 7" ....$375.00 – 450.00
5. Earlam, 6½" ....$900.00 – 1,000.00

Row 3:
1. Imperial II, 6½" ....$900.00 – 1,000.00
2. Imperial II, 6½" ....$1,750.00 – 2,000.00
3. Imperial II, 6½" ....$700.00 – 800.00
4. Imperial II, 6½" ....$700.00 – 800.00

Row 4:
1. Dahlrose, 10" ....$450.00 – 550.00
2. Rosecraft Panel, 7" ....$750.00 – 850.00
3. Rosecraft Panel, 9" ....$400.00 – 450.00
4. Rosecraft Panel, 9" ....$450.00 – 500.00

Page 184, Wall Pockets
Row 1:
1. Blackberry, 8½" ....$2,000.00 – 2,500.00
2. Sunflower, 7½" ....$2,000.00 – 2,500.00
3. Wisteria, 8", tan.......................$1,500.00 – 1,750.00
   blue ....$1,750.00 – 2,000.00

Row 2:
1. Velmoss, 8½", green ....$2,000.00 – 2,250.00
   red, blue or tan......................$2,500.00 – 2,750.00
2. Ferella, 6½", pink ....$2,000.00 – 2,500.00
   brown ....$1,750.00 – 2,000.00
3. Baneda, 8", pink ....$3,500.00 – 4,000.00
   green ....$3,000.00 – 3,500.00
4. Jonquil, 8½" ....$900.00 – 1,000.00
5. Morning Glory, 8½", green...............$1,500.00 – 1,750.00
   white................................$1,250.00 – 1,500.00

Row 3:
1. Cherry Blossom, 8", pink.................$1,500.00 – 1,750.00
   brown ....$800.00 – 1,000.00
2. Thorn Apple bucket, 8½"................$1,250.00 – 1,500.00
3. Moss bucket, 10" ....$750.00 – 850.00
4. Luffa, 8½"...........................$900.00 – 1,000.00

Row 4:
1. Thorn Apple, 8", #1280-8 ....$700.00 – 800.00
2. Orian, 8" ....$1,000.00 – 1,200.00
3. Moss, 8", #1278-8 ....$750.00 – 850.00

Page 185, Wall Pockets, Plates, Shelves
Row 1:
1. Peony, 8", #1293-8 ....$400.00 – 450.00
2. Iris, 8", #1284-8 ....$750.00 – 850.00
3. Fuchsia, 8½", #1282-8, blue...........$1,000.00 – 1,200.00
   brown or green......................$750.00 – 850.00
4. Bleeding Heart, 8½", #1287-8 ....$650.00 – 750.00

Row 2:
1. Primrose, 8½", #1277-8, blue.............$800.00 – 900.00

45

tan or pink..$675.00 – 750.00
  2. Poppy, 8½", #1281-8, pink.................$900.00 – 1,000.00
     gray or green...................................$750.00 – 850.00
  3. Cosmos, 8½", #1286-8, blue or green ...$750.00 – 850.00
     tan...$650.00 – 725.00

Row 3:
  1. Pine Cone, 8½", #466, blue.................. $750.00 – 850.00
     brown...$650.00 – 725.00
     green..$575.00 – 625.00
  2. Pine Cone plate, 7½, blue ....$850.00 – 950.00
     brown...$700.00 – 750.00
     green..$600.00 – 650.00
  3. Pine Cone bucket, 9", #1283, blue...$1,200.00 – 1,400.00
     brown...$750.00 – 850.00
     green..$850.00 – 950.00

Row 4:
  1. Pine Cone wall shelf, #1, blue ....$750.00 – 850.00
     brown...$550.00 – 650.00
     green..$650.00 – 750.00
  2. Pine Cone, 8½", #1273-8, blue ....$750.00 – 850.00
     brown...$550.00 – 650.00
     green..$450.00 – 525.00
  3. Ivory II, 8½", #1273-8.........................$450.00 – 550.00
  4. Ivory shelf, 5½", #8............................$175.00 – 225.00

Page 186, Wall Pockets
Row 1:
  1. Florentine, 7"..................................$150.00 – 175.00
  2. Florentine, 9½"................................$250.00 – 275.00
  3. Dahlrose, 9" ....$225.00 – 275.00
  4. Imperial I, 8" ....$350.00 – 425.00

Row 2:
     Wincraft, 5", #267-5...........................$250.00 – 300.00

Row 3:
  1. Dogwood I, 10" ....$600.00 – 700.00
  2. Carnelian II, 7"................................$550.00 – 650.00
  3. Tuscany, 8"....................................$375.00 – 450.00
  4. Velmoss Scroll, 11½" ....$400.00 – 475.00

Row 4:
  1. Chloron, 10½" ....$350.00 – 400.00
  2. Mayfair, 8", #1014-8.........................$250.00 – 300.00
  3. Mostique, 10½"...............................$350.00 – 400.00

Row 5:
  1. White Rose, 6½", #1288-6....................$350.00 – 400.00
  2. Capri, 5", #1013-5 ....$500.00 – 600.00
  3. Lotus, 7½", #L8-7 ....$400.00 – 475.00
  4. Wincraft, 8½", #266-4........................$250.00 – 300.00
  5. Cosmos, 6½", #1285 ....$350.00 – 400.00

Page 187, Wall Pockets
Row 1:
  1. Gardenia, 9½", #666-8........................$350.00 – 400.00
  2. Foxglove, 8", #1292-8 ....$450.00 – 500.00
  3. Columbine, 8½", #1290-8.....................$750.00 – 800.00
  4. Freesia, 8½", #1296-8........................$250.00 – 300.00

Row 2:
  1. Apple Blossom, 8½", #366-8.................$300.00 – 350.00
  2. Zephyr Lily, 8", #1297-8, prototype original ....NPA
     standard glazes................................$300.00 – 350.00
  3. Magnolia, 8½", #1294.........................$300.00 – 350.00
  4. Bittersweet, 7½", #866-7.....................$300.00 – 350.00

Row 3:
  1. White Rose, 8½", #1289-8.....................$450.00 – 500.00
  2. Snowberry, 8", #1WP-8.......................$225.00 – 275.00
  3. Clematis, 8½", #1295-8.......................$225.00 – 275.00
  4. Bushberry, 8", #1291-8, orange.............$350.00 – 425.00
     blue..$450.00 – 525.00
     green..$400.00 – 475.00

Row 4:
  1. Silhouette, 8", #766-8 ....$275.00 – 350.00
  2. Burmese, 7½", #72-B, green glaze........$250.00 – 275.00
  3. Burmese, 7½", #82-B, white glaze ....$250.00 – 275.00
  4. Ming Tree, 8½", #566-8 ....$375.00 – 450.00

Page 188, Trials
  1. "Serra," 6".....................................$375.00 – 450.00
  2. Pine Cone, 9"..................................$750.00 – 900.00
  3. Vase, 9".....................................$2,500.00 – 3,000.00
  4. Mock Orange, 8", #974-8 ....$450.00 – 550.00
  5. Decorated Imperial II, 5" ....$850.00 – 950.00

Page 189, Experimentals
Row 1:
  1. Freesia design, 9" ....$4,000.00 – 5,000.00
  2. Gladiola design ....$4,000.00 – 5,000.00
  3. Lupines design ....$4,000.00 – 5,000.00

Row 2:
  1. Black Eyed Susan ....$3,000.00 – 3,500.00
  2. Orchid.......................................$6,000.00 – 7,000.00
  3. Blackberry ....$6,000.00 – 7,000.00

Row 3:
  1. White Rose design..........................$4,000.00 – 5,000.00
  2. Bittersweet ....$4,000.00 – 5,000.00
  3. Geranium....................................$4,000.00 – 5,000.00

Row 4:
  1. Arrowhead design ....$3,000.00 – 3,500.00
  2. Arrowhead design ....$4,000.00 – 5,000.00
  3. Larkspur design ....$4,000.00 – 5,000.00

Page 190, Experimentals
Row 1:
  1. Pine Cone design, 6" ....$2,500.00 – 3,000.00
  2. Pine Cone design, 8" ....$2,500.00 – 3,000.00
  3. Vase, 5".....................................$1,250.00 – 1,500.00

Row 2:
  1. Nude, 10" ....$3,500.00 – 4,500.00
  2. Nude, 10" ....$2,000.00 – 2,750.00
  3. Nude, 10" ....$3,500.00 – 4,500.00

Row 3:
1. Nude, 12½" ....$5,000.00 – 6,000.00
2. Pine Cone design, 20½" ....$6,000.00 – 7,500.00
3. Dogwood design, 16½" ....$6,000.00 – 7,500.00

Page 191, Experimentals
Row 1:
1. Primrose design, 10" ....$4,500.00 – 5,500.00
2. Sweet Syringa or Mock Orange, 8½"..$3,500.00 – 4,000.00
3. Floral design, 8" ....$2,000.00 – 2,500.00
4. Floral design, 10" ....$3,000.00 – 3,750.00

Row 2:
1. Gladiola design, 9½"..........................$2,000.00 – 2,500.00
2. Bittersweet design, 13" ....$1,000.00 – 1,250.00
3. Arrowhead design, 13" ....$1,000.00 – 1,250.00
4. Freesia design, 8½" ....$2,000.00 – 2,500.00

Trials, Experimentals
Row 1:
8" Plates, each.......................................$350.00 – 450.00

Row 2:
1. Planter, 3"...$150.00 – 200.00
2. Ming Tree, 8" ....$700.00 – 800.00
3. Window box, 3½" x 10", tan to blue ......$250.00 – 300.00

Row 3:
1. Laurel, 8" ....$900.00 – 1,000.00
2. Wild Rose, 10" ....$2,500.00 – 3,500.00
3. Vase, 8½" ....$475.00 – 550.00
4. Moderne, 8", $796-8.........................$600.00 – 700.00

Page 192, Trials, Experimentals
Row 1: (Trials)
1. Tulip vase, 6", #1001-6 ....$300.00 – 400.00
2. Savona, 6"...$450.00 – 550.00
3. Baneda, 6" ....$900.00 – 1,000.00
4. "New Colors" incised on base, 7" ....$250.00 – 350.00
5. Cherry Blossom bowl, 4" ....$850.00 – 950.00

Row 2:
1. Morning Glory, 8" ....$1,000.00 – 1,250.00
2. Morning Glory ....$1,000.00 – 1,250.00
3. Morning Glory ....$1,000.00 – 1,250.00

Row 3:
1. Cherry Blossom, 7" ....$2,500.00 – 3,500.00
2. Cosmos over Teasel blank, 8", #884 $2,000.00 – 2,500.00
3. Freesia design, 7" ....$2,000.00 – 2,500.00
4. Stylized Honeysuckle, 6½" ....$1,250.00 – 1,500.00
Row 4:
1. Floral design, 8" ....$4,000.00 – 5,000.00
2. Wild Grape design, 9½"....................$3,000.00 – 4,000.00
3. Cherry Blossom design, 7" ....$4,000.00 – 5,000.00

Page 193, Victorian Art Pottery
Vase, 11" ....$3,000.00 – 4,000.00

Trials, Experimentals
Plates, each ....$350.00 – 450.00

Lamps
1. Base, 11½"...$400.00 – 500.00
2. Imperial II, 5" ....$1,000.00 – 1,200.00
3. Base, 12"..$900.00 – 1,000.00
4. Base, 8½"..$450.00 – 550.00

Page 194, Lamps
Row 1:
1. Imperial II base, 8", #34-4 ....$800.00 – 900.00
2. Imperial II base, 8", #F39-4 ....$800.00 – 900.00

Row 2:
1. Base, 7"...$350.00 – 400.00
2. Base, 10", #F84-R7 ....$1,000.00 – 1,250.00
3. Ixia base, 7½" ....$600.00 – 700.00

Row 3:
1. Base, 8½"..$400.00 – 450.00
2. Base, 10½"..$1,000.00 – 1,250.00
3. Base, 5½"..$650.00 – 750.00

Radiator cover, set made exclusively for
Russell T. Young...NPA

Page 195, Umbrella Stands
1. Blended Basketweave, 21"....................$250.00 – 350.00
2. #701 Blended, 22" ....$250.00 – 350.00
3. #734 Blended, 21" ....$250.00 – 350.00

1. #132 Blended, 21½" ....$400.00 – 500.00
2. #705 Blended Stork, 19" ....$375.00 – 450.00
3. #719 Blended 22" ....$400.00 – 450.00

Page 196, Jardinieres and Pedestals
1. #126 Blended, 29½" ....$400.00 – 500.00
2. Matt Green, 36" ....$3,500.00 – 4,000.00
3. Decorated Creamware, 29" ....$750.00 – 1,000.00

1. Ivory Florentine, 29" ....$1,250.00 – 1,500.00
2. Ivory Cameo, 34", #439 ....$1,500.00 – 2,000.00
3. Rozane 1917, 28½" ....$850.00 – 950.00

Page 197, Jardinieres and Pedestals, Umbrella Stand
1. Decorated Landscape, 43" ....$5,000.00 – 6,000.00
2. Umbrella stand, 22" ....$2,500.00 – 3,000.00
3. Decorated Landscape, 44" ....$5,000.00 – 6,000.00

1. #451 Blended Iris, 31" ....$750.00 – 850.00
2. #441 Blended, 38" ....$800.00 – 900.00
3. #414 Blended, 28" ....$750.00 – 850.00

Page 198 Umbrella Stands
1. Gold and Silver Decorated, 22½" .....$1,250.00 – 1,500.00
2. Decorated Matt, 20", #724 ....$5,000.00 – 6,000.00
3. Gold and Silver Decorated, 21½" .....$1,250.00 – 1,500.00

Jardinieres and Pedestals
1. Early Ceramic, 49" ....$3,000.00 – 3,500.00
2. Fleur De Lis, 20½", #412 ....$500.00 – 600.00

PRICE GUIDE — VOLUME 2, REVISED EDITION

Page 199, Umbrella Stands
1. Normandy, 20" ....$750.00 – 850.00
2. Tourist, 22½" ....$5,000.00 – 6,000.00
3. Corinthian, 20" ....$750.00 – 800.00

Jardinieres and Pedestals
1. Donatello, 34" ....$1,250.00 – 1,500.00
2. Rosecraft Vintage, 30½" ....$1,250.00 – 1,500.00
3. Corinthian, 30½" ....$1,000.00 – 1,200.00

Sand Jars, Urn, Umbrella Stand
1. Ivory II sand jar, 14½" ....$300.00 – 400.00
2. Ivory Florentine urn, 16½", #297 ....$400.00 – 500.00
3. Ivory Florentine umbrella stands,
   18½", #298....................................$350.00 – 450.00
4. Normandy sand jar, 14" ....$750.00 – 850.00

Page 200, Jardinieres and Pedestals
1. Decorated Creamware, 26" ....$850.00 – 1,000.00
2. Rozane, 28", #516 ....$1,000.00 – 1,250.00
3. Florentine, 25"...............................$800.00 – 1,000.00
4. Wisteria, 24½" ....$2,500.00 – 3,000.00
   blue ....$3,500.00 – 4,000.00

Rozane Floor Vases
1. Vase, 25", #850-3 ....$3,000.00 – 3,500.00
2. Vase, 29½"..................................$4,000.00 – 5,000.00
3. Vase, 20", #632............................$2,500.00 – 3,000.00

Page 201, Jardinieres and Pedestals
1. Donatello, 23½" ....$1,000.00 – 1,250.00
2. Artcraft, 24½"................................$2,000.00 – 2,250.00
3. Cherry Blossom, 25½", brown..........$2,500.00 – 3,000.00
   pink ....$3,500.00 – 4,500.00
4. Corinthian, 24" ....$650.00 – 750.00

1. Artcraft, 28"...................................$4,000.00 – 4,500.00
2. Blackberry, 28".............................$3,500.00 – 4,000.00
3. Dahlrose, 30½" ....$1,800.00 – 2,250.00

Page 202, Jardinieres and Pedestals
1. Dogwood II, 30" ....$1,000.00 – 1,200.00
2. Rozane 1917, 35" ....$1,250.00 – 1,500.00
3. Vista, 28"......................................$3,500.00 – 4,500.00

1. Jonquil, 29" ....$2,500.00 – 3,000.00
2. Normandy, 28" ....$1,000.00 – 1,200.00
3. Sunflower, 29"..............................$4,500.00 – 5,500.00

Page 203, Umbrella Stand, Jardinieres and Pedestals
1. #720 Matt Green umbrella stand, 23"$1,250.00 – 1,500.00
2. Peony jardiniere & pedestal, 30", #661$1,750.00 – 2,000.00
3. Blended Mostique jardiniere &
   pedestal, 27½" ....$500.00 – 750.00

Umbrella Stands
1. #727 blended, 20" ....$250.00 – 350.00
2. Earlam, 20", #741 ....$3,000.00 – 4,000.00
3. #609 Blended, 20" ....$275.00 – 375.00

Page 204, Jardinieres and Pedestals
1. Foxglove, 30½", #659 on jardiniere,
   green ....$2,000.00 – 2,500.00
   blue ....$1,750.00 – 2,250.00
   pink ....$1,500.00 – 1,750.00
2. Rosecraft Blended, 28"....................$1,000.00 – 1,250.00

1. Snowberry, 25", #1P8 U.S.A. on ped;
   #1J8 on jard ....$1,000.00 – 1,100.00
2. Luffa, 24½"................................$1,750.00 – 2,000.00
3. La Rose, 24½" ....$1,000.00 – 1,200.00
4. Zephyr Lily, 25", #671-8, blue...........$1,000.00 – 1,200.00
   brown ....$850.00 – 950.00
   green ....$750.00 – 850.00

Page 205, Assorted Floor Pieces
1. Earlam sand jar, 12½" ....$1,250.00 –1,500.00
2. Carnelian I floor vase, 18½"..................$500.00 – 600.00
3. Ming Tree floor vase, 15½", #586-15 .....$550.00 – 650.00
4. #708 Blended umbrella stand, 19½" ......$350.00 – 450.00
5. Florane, late line, sand jar, 12", #52-12..$100.00 – 150.00

Umbrella Stands
1. Bushberry, 20½", #779-20, blue.......$1,250.00 – 1,500.00
   green ....$1,000.00 – 1,100.00
   orange ....$800.00 – 900.00
2. Sunflower, 20½"............................$4,000.00 – 5,000.00
3. Dogwood I, 19½" ....$1,000.00 – 1,200.00